The Christian Conundrum

Todd D. Bennett

Shema Yisrael Publications

The Christian Conundrum
First printing 2016

Copyright © 2016 by Shema Yisrael Publications. All rights reserved. No part of this book may be used or reproduced in any manner whatsoever without written permission of the publisher, except in the case of brief quotations in articles and reviews.

ISBN: 978-0-9863032-0-3
Library of Congress Control Number: 2016901744

Printed in the United States of America.

Please visit our website for other titles:
www.shemayisrael.net

For information write:
Shema Yisrael Publications
123 Court Street
Herkimer, New York 13350

For information regarding publicity for author interviews call
(866) 866-2211

The Christian Conundrum

Todd D. Bennett

"*⁸ Behold, you trust in lying words that cannot profit. ⁹ Will you steal, murder, commit adultery, swear falsely, burn incense to Baal, and walk after other gods whom you do not know, ¹⁰ and then come and stand before Me in this house which is called by My Name, and say, 'We are delivered! Only to go on doing all these abominations?'"*

Jeremiah 7:8-10

Table of Contents

Chapter 1	Religion	1
Chapter 2	The Law	11
Chapter 3	The Messiah	29
Chapter 4	But Paul Said …	53
Chapter 5	Amazing Grace	64
Chapter 6	Christianity	73
Chapter 7	Lawlessness	93
Chapter 8	All You Need Is Love	110
Chapter 9	The Conundrum	119
The Walk in the Light Series		134
The Shema		136

I

Religion

Every religion has a system of beliefs that separate it from other religions. They each consider their faith to constitute truth. The ultimate question is which religion actually contains and promotes truth, because all of them cannot be right. Further, most religions in the world are internally divided into different sects due to varied interpretations of their underlying texts and the words of their prophets, priests, rabbis, mahdis or gurus. Sometimes these rifts are so severe that they lead to different sects, within the same faith, killing one another.

I was born a Christian and immersed in Christian culture and tradition all of my life. I read my Bible, prayed daily, and regularly attended Church. I believed in God and I believed in His Word. I still do, although not the same as I used to because I discovered a conundrum that exists in the Christian religion.

I was raised in a traditional mainstream denomination that stressed the inerrancy of the Bible as the Word of God. The problem I discovered was that the traditions and accepted beliefs of the denomination did not always synchronize with the texts that supposedly underpinned the faith. This seeming contradiction did not diminish my belief in God, but it did leave me with many unanswered and lingering questions regarding my religion.

Now, many Christians do not read their Bibles so the problem is not evident to them. They go to church on

Sunday, listen to the sermons taught from the pulpit, sing their songs, and all is well. They follow the traditions of Christianity and many do not even understand how their particular denomination differs from other Christian denominations.

I grew up in a small town that had four different Christian Church buildings on four street corners all within a stone's throw of one another. As a child, I never understood why they were separated from each other. Even now, I fail to see how the seemingly minor doctrinal differences could cause people of the same religion to be so divided.

Over time it became very clear to me that it was not the Bible that divided these denominations, but rather the interpretations and the traditions that these denominations clung to. The Bible is very clear - if you do not read it through a denominational lens.

The sad and painful reality is that tradition often trumps truth or provides the framework for people's understanding, which is the exact opposite of how it should be. You see, our traditions should not determine truth, rather truth should determine our traditions. This occurs because traditions get ingrained within our lives and our culture to the point where we sometimes cannot distinguish between a tradition and truth.

For instance, Christians follow the tradition of celebrating the birth of Christ on December 25th. There is nothing in the Bible that says the birth of Jesus occurred on December 25th. In fact, there is significant evidence that the birth of the Messiah[1] occurred on a special Scriptural Appointed Time known as the Day of

---

[1] I use the word Messiah rather than Christ because it derives from the Hebrew word "moshiach." It refers to the very specific and anticipated One described in the Hebrew Scriptures while the word "christ" has been applied to many pagan savior gods.

Trumpets.[2]

Further, it is crystal clear that the December 25th tradition traces back to pagan sun worship, when people celebrated the death and rebirth of the sun on the winter solstice.[3]

Regardless of this irrefutable evidence that can certainly be classified as truth, Christianity follows a tradition. Some who recognize the contradiction see it as harmless error and many proclaim: "Hey, we have to celebrate the birth of Jesus some time, so why not Christmas?" The problem with that logic is that they have chosen a date when all pagans celebrate the birth of their savior sun gods. This practice directly defies the mandate found in the Bible not to worship the Creator as the pagans worship their false gods.[4]

Remember when the Israelites constructed a golden calf at the base of Mount Sinai? They said that they were doing it for God.[5] That is exactly what Christians are doing when they celebrate Christmas. They are adopting pagan traditions and are incorporating them into the worship of the Creator. This is not harmless error.

Again, this is expressly forbidden in the Bible, but most Christians either do not know, or they do not care. In either case, they will be held to account for their actions. The Creator clearly instructs us how to worship Him. He repeatedly commands us to seek Him and serve

---

[2] The Day of Trumpets, also known as the Day of Blasting, is Yom Teruah in Hebrew. It occurs on Day 1 of Month 7 on the Scriptural Calendar. The Scriptural Calendar and the Appointed Times are discussed in depth in the Walk in the Light series book entitled *Appointed Times*.

[3] The winter solstice currently falls on December 21st due to the procession of the equinoxes. The ancient worship of the sun traces back to ancient Babylon at a time when the winter solstice fell on December 25th. This date also shifted due to the change from the Julian Calendar to the Gregorian Calendar, but the essential purpose in celebrating the December 25th date derives from sun worship. Through the process known as syncrotism, the Christian religion adapted and included the pagan practice to attract and keep new pagan converts.

[4] Deuteronomy 12:2-4, 29-31

[5] Exodus 32:5

Him diligently and He gives us specific times to assemble and worship Him.[6]

This is a simple example of the power of tradition; and Christmas is just one of many traditions that I learned in Church which does not reconcile with the Bible. Since I was taught to believe that the Bible is the inerrant Word of God, it became evident to me that my religion did not always follow the Bible.

So it comes down to a choice. We all have a decision to make. You must decide whether you desire to follow truth or tradition. What is more important to you – your religion or your Creator? If and when these two conflict with one another, you must determine whether you will follow the traditions of your religion or the Commandments of the Creator. If you choose the Creator then you must follow Him and obey Him at all cost, even if it means rejecting your inherited religion, denomination or tradition.

This is why Messiah said: "*If anyone comes to Me and does not hate his father and mother, wife and children, brothers and sisters, yes, and his own life also, he cannot be My disciple.*" (Luke 14:26). He was stressing the point that the only way that the people could truly follow Him was by giving up the traditions learned and reinforced by family. He came and taught in a time when religious traditions had led men astray from the truth. He spent much time exposing the hypocrisy of the religious teachers as they taught their traditions over the Commandments.

In an incident involving the tradition concerning the washing of hands He stated: "*All too well you reject the Commandment of God, that you may keep your **tradition**.*" (Mark 7:9). How true this statement was then concerning the Pharisees and how true it is now concerning the Christian religion. Christianity has actually committed the same sin as the Pharisees by

---

[6] See Leviticus 23 for a summary of the Appointed Times.

rejecting the Commandments and keeping their traditions.

Now this may sound shocking to a Christian reader. After all, most Christians are taught that Jesus came to do away with the Law and start the religion of Christianity and the Christian Church. This is an important paradigm taught in Christianity that completely flies in the face of all of the Scriptures.

The Messiah was a Yisraelite[7] from the Tribe of Judah. He specifically said that He did not come to abolish the Law[8] and He also specifically said that He came for the "lost sheep of the house of Yisrael."[9] He did not come to start a new religion, but rather to renew the Covenant that had been broken by the house of Yisrael. This is described in the Bible and repeatedly foretold by the prophets. Unfortunately, it is a very foreign concept to Christians who have been taught a warped paradigm that completely skews the way that they read about, and understand the plan of the Creator.

This only becomes clear if you take off your religious filter and proceed to read and study the Scriptures without any traditional or doctrinal bias. This is what ultimately happened to me. There came a time when I stepped outside of my religious construct and started interpreting the passages of the Scriptures within their original language and context. This process helped me to accurately see not only the plan of the Creator, but also how I fit into that plan.

As already mentioned, I actually read my Bible

---

[7] The word Yisraelite refers to one who is a member of the Covenant Assembly of Yisrael. This is not the same as the modern State of Israel, but rather the 12 Tribes that descended from the man Jacob, renamed Yisrael, along with all those who joined into the Covenant.

[8] "*Do not think that I came to destroy the Law or the Prophets. I did not come to destroy but to fulfill. [18] For assuredly, I say to you, till heaven and earth pass away, one jot or one tittle will by no means pass from the law till all is fulfilled.*" Matthew 5:17

[9] "*But He answered and said, 'I was not sent except to the lost sheep of the house of Israel.'*" Matthew 15:24

many times over as a youth and I was always perplexed when I was told that the Creator had given Commandments to Yisrael that no longer applied to Christians.

The Scriptures described Yisrael as a Bride and the Creator as a Husband.[10] Yisrael was called not only to be a Bride in a Covenant relationship with the Creator, but also a nation of Priests who lived and taught righteousness to the heathen nations. As these Covenant people followed the Commandments, they lived and learned righteous behavior, and they were to be blessed. The Commandments are righteousness. This is clearly expressed in the Scriptures. *"My tongue shall speak of Your Word, for all Your commandments are righteousness."* (Psalm 119:172).

For some reason, I was always led to believe that the Commandments were difficult and led to bondage and oppression. This was a tradition that specifically contradicted Moses who said they were not too difficult for Yisrael to obey.[11] In fact, if you actually take the time to sit down and read the Commandments, you will find that they are very basic and that they instruct us on how to relate to God, how to treat our neighbor, how to handle civil disputes and even criminal matters.

They also detail acceptable sexual behavior and even provide the definition for food. In essence, they are the instructions for a righteous people to live well and dwell together with a Holy God on Earth. This life on Earth is simply a training period for those who desire to dwell with God eternally in His heavenly Kingdom.

The Commandments are the same now as they were in the past. The question is whether or not you will obey them now. I used to ponder why some of these Commandments were considered irrelevant to

---

[10] Jeremiah 31:32
[11] Deuteronomy 30:11

Christians while others were not. It seemed that people would cherry pick the Commandments and then argue why some applied and why some did not, usually due to some advent, change or other arbitrary reason.

For example, the Scriptures provide very precise information regarding what is food that is fit to be eaten versus what is unacceptable for consumption. I could never understand why pig could not be eaten by the Yisraelites, the people chosen by God to represent Him as priests to the world, but it was perfectly acceptable for Christians to eat something He called an abomination.[12] This was especially compelling to me since most Christians believe that they have replaced Yisrael, or that they are "spiritual Yisrael." So, why wouldn't they eat like Yisrael?

This was also disconcerting to me because according to Christian tradition, ancient Yisrael was apparently given Commandments that they could not obey and then punished for failing to obey. Amazingly, also according to Christian tradition, the Christian Church has apparently replaced Yisrael as the chosen people and now they don't even have to obey the Commandments.

Talk about a great deal for the Christians and what a raw deal for those Yisraelites! This does not sound like something a loving God would do. It not only sounds unfair, but also cruel.[13]

---

[12] Leviticus 11:1-11 and Deuteronomy 14:8
[13] This schizophrenic representation of the Creator derives from a heretic named Marcion. Marcion of Sinope lived between 85 CE and 160 CE. He was the Bishop of a heretical religious sect referred to as the Marcionites. He taught a dualist belief system - that the god of the Old Testament was a separate and distinct god from the New Testament. As a result, he emphasized various texts over the Old Testament and essentially threw out the foundation of the faith. Because of the destructive nature of his false teachings, many attribute the decision to develop the canon of the New Testament to Marcion. The development of the canon of the New Testament was essentially an attempt to solidify orthodox doctrine and agree upon texts that supported that doctrine. Prior to that time, various letters and Gospels were circulating amongst the Assemblies, and were not treated as Scriptures.

When I posed this question of unfairness and inconsistency to Christian leaders, I was typically given some terse response such as there was no longer a Temple so those laws did not apply. There was never any real thought put into the question or the answer, but simply a knee jerk response based upon their inherited religious paradigm that Christians do not have to obey the Commandments.

Of course, the notion that Christians are immune from obeying the Commandments is really absurd, if you put just a moment of thought into the issue. It is clearly not OK to murder, steal, commit adultery, practice incest, bestiality or witchcraft. These are all Commandments found in the Bible that we can clearly obey, along with many others that are quite necessary for any moral, decent, God-fearing society.

It is really not hard to stop eating swine, and there are, in fact, health benefits associated with refraining from pig consumption. It actually comes down to a decision to follow the Commandments or follow the appetites and lusts of the flesh.

This is the plight of mankind that traces back to the Garden of Eden. In fact, man's current fallen state stems specifically from the fact that man sinned in the Garden of Eden and was expelled. Therefore, isn't it our problem that we have sinned and isn't sin defined as a violation of the Commandments? Of course, every Christian would answer these questions in the affirmative. They would also agree that the Messiah came and died so that our sins could be forgiven. So then does it make sense that after receiving forgiveness we would then continue in a life of sin? Of course not!

In fact, the author of Hebrews put it this way: "[26] *For if we sin willfully after we have received the knowledge of the truth, there no longer remains a sacrifice for sins,* [27] *but a certain fearful expectation of judgment, and fiery indignation* which will devour the adversaries. ²⁸ Anyone who has rejected Moses' law dies without mercy on the testimony of two or three witnesses. ²⁹ Of how much worse punishment, do you suppose, will he be thought worthy who has trampled the Son of God underfoot, counted the blood of the Covenant by which he was sanctified a common thing, and insulted the Spirit of grace?" Hebrews 10:26-29

This passage ends with a question that most Christians are remiss to answer because it describes exactly what the majority of Christians are doing. They have been taught that they cannot or should not obey the Commandments because by doing so they will be put under bondage when the exact opposite is true. You are in bondage and a slave to sin when you live a sinful life - a life of lawlessness. The Commandments actually provide freedom from the slavery caused by sin. That is why James referred to the Commandments as "*the perfect law of liberty.*"[14]

The irony is that a life of obedience leads to blessings and sets you free from the bondage of sin and the resultant curses. That is what the Bible teaches, yet popular Christian tradition tends to contradict this clear precept.

Ultimately, the fallback position for most Christians is Paul. The strongest arguments against obeying the Commandments always seem to come from one of the letters written by Paul. That really gets to the heart of the matter because we actually have written documents, included in the New Testament, that either directly contradict or appear to contradict, something in the Old Testament. Faced with this apparent dilemma every person has a choice to make. Will you follow the clear and overwhelming thrust of the Scriptures by obeying the Commandments or will you reject the Commandments because of a letter, sentence or phrase

---

[14] James 1:25 see also James 2:12

written by a man?

    This is at the heart of the paradox that I call the Christian Conundrum. While Christians carry their Bibles as one text, apparently consisting of the inerrant word of God, how can it contradict itself? This is especially true when God specifically states that He does not change.[15]

    The "Old" versus "New" paradigm comes down to a conflict created between the Law and Grace – a conflict that does not need to exist. In order to better comprehend this conflict, it is important to first understand what is commonly referred to as The Law.

---

[15] Malachi 3:6

2

The Law

Language and translations are extremely powerful and important to our understanding of the Scriptures and our walk of faith. A good translation can help us better understand a concept or Commandment, and a bad translation can be utterly destructive.

We already spoke of the idea that the Bible is the inerrant Word of God. That is a presumption commonly professed and proclaimed throughout Christianity without much clarification or support. When considering the notion of inerrancy you must first ask which text or compilation of texts is inerrant, and then consider the source language and any subsequent translation of the text. This is a multilayered and complicated process.

We know that none of the Biblical texts originated in English, Spanish or any other modern language for that matter. So most Bibles are translations from another language, and most Christians would be shocked to know that we do not have original manuscripts of any Biblical texts.

Prior to the discovery of the Dead Sea Scrolls the oldest copy of the Old Testament was around 1,000 years old. The Dead Sea Scrolls provided texts that were approximately 1,000 years older than that. Some of those "Dead Sea Scrolls" were actually discovered in scroll form, but most of them are simply fragments. They were an incredible find because we were able to discern the accuracy of the Old Testament Hebrew texts that we had been using up to that point.

The New Testament texts are a very different

issue. There are no Hebrew New Testament texts found, although there is a strong suspicion that some were originally written in Hebrew or Aramaic. In fact, there is a large body of Aramiac texts dating back to the 12th century that are largely ignored by most Bible translators.[16]

Thus, most modern English Bibles are translated from the Greek language, rather than Hebrew or Aramaic. There are thousands of fragments of the Greek texts and prior to the development of the "textus receptus," known as "the received text," there was no uniform New Testament. It was not until the 1500s that much work was done to compile a unified text for the sake of printing Bibles and developing a received text was the work of many individuals.[17]

When I grew up as a youth and heard the professions of inerrancy proclaimed from the pulpit, I was led to believe that the Holy Spirit selected each and every text to be included in the Bible. It was implied, if not directly stated, that the Spirit fell upon each author of each text and guided their hands as they wrote each word under the direct inspiration of God.

Now while we know that it happened with Moses, it is not so clear how all of the other texts of the Bible came into existence. And that is what makes the particular texts written by Moses so special. The Scriptures record that Moses *"wrote all the words"* that were given to Him on Sinai.[18]

Remember that it was God Who wrote the Words on the stone tablets that He had spoken from the mountain, but it was Moses who wrote all the words that

---

[16] A very good New Testament translation deriving from the Eastern Peshitta family of texts, including the Khabouris Codex, is the Aramaic English New Testament (AENT) translated by Andrew Gabriel Roth.
[17] The compilation of the Bible is discussed further in the Walk in the Light series book entitled *The Scriptures*.
[18] Exodus 24:4

were given to him when He went up the mountain. The words written by Moses are known as the Book of the Law, or rather, the Scroll of the Covenant.

This Scroll of the Covenant was apparently a work in progress throughout his life as we read the following words immediately prior to his death:

"[24] So it was, when Moses had completed writing the words of this law in a book, when they were finished, [25] that Moses commanded the Levites, who bore the ark of the covenant of the LORD, saying: [26] 'Take this Book of the Law, and put it beside the Ark of the Covenant of the LORD your God, that it may be there as a witness against you.'"
Deuteronomy 31:24-26

Now this passage is a popular English translation of a Hebrew text and it is not accurately translated. You can probably guess one mistake right away. The word "book" is "sepher" (ספר) in Hebrew and it means "scroll." There were no codex books at the time and people wrote on scrolls. That was an easy one.

Another translation issue involves the title and Name of the Creator. The Creator has a Name that occurs almost 7,000 times in the Hebrew Scriptures, but rarely is that Name ever revealed in a translated text. Instead, the Name is hidden behind a title such as "The LORD," found in some English Bibles.

It is obvious that "the LORD" is not a name. Rather, it is a title that the English translators use to replace the Hebrew Name of the Creator. The Name of the Creator is depicted in the modern Hebrew as יהוה and the Ancient Script as 𐤉𐤄𐤅𐤄. The Hebrew language consists of 22 characters, originally written as pictographs. Each pictograph has a meaning and by combining them together they form words with meanings.

Most people who read a translation of the Bible are unaware of the rich content contained in the original language. They also fail to understand that translators have fallen short in completely transmitting the contents of the original texts - primarily because of language differences.[19]

For instance, the English and Hebrew languages read in the opposite directions. While English reads from left to right, the Hebrew reads from right to left. This simple difference actually has profound effects on the cultures and the thought processes of those who communicate in these "opposite" languages.[20]

The original ancient Hebrew language consisted of consonants. The vowel sounds are generally not represented by characters in the original text. Therefore the Hebrew Name of the Creator consists of four consonants yud (י), hey (ה), vav (ו), hey (ה) that read from right to left. In order to achieve an English equivalent of the Name we use the English consonants Y (י), H (ה), W(ו), H(ה). Thus in English we represent it from left to right as YHWH, but in Hebrew it reads from right to left יהוה.[21]

We do this in order to get to the proper pronunciation. While there are traditions that claim that the Name is ineffable or unspeakable, that is simply not true. Some commonly accepted pronunciations of the

---

[19] This statement in not intended to be a knock against translators. All of us who were not raised in the Hebrew language and culture owe a great debt of gratitude for translators who have made the texts readable to those of other languages. The point is to recognize their limitations and attempt to discern when the translations fall short. This may be a difficult truth for someone raised on a particular English translation believing that it is the "inerrant Word of God." This subject is discussed in greater detail in the Walk in the Light series book entitled *The Scriptures*.

[20] See *Hebrew Thought Compared to Greek*, Thorleif Boman, W. W. Norton & Company (1970).

[21] It is important to remember that the Hebrew language reads from right to left. When providing the Name as English consonants it reads from left to right. This is only done to aid the reader in recognizing and pronouncing the Name. It is not intended to replace the Hebrew Name that always reads from right to left.

Name of the Creator are Yahuwah or Yehowah.²² Since the pronunciation is a disputed issue the Name will be presented as YHWH through the remainder of this book.

This Name was hidden from me my entire life just beneath the translation of my English Bible. Indeed, due to these translation traditions the Name is hidden from almost the entire world. Even Jews who maintain their Scriptures in the modern Hebrew language traditionally do not speak the Name, but in fact replace the Name with the title "Adonai" or "Hashem." They supposedly do this for the sake of piety, but the Scriptures are clear that YHWH wants the world to know Him. That is why He revealed His Name in a language that can be spoken.

It is hard to know someone or have an intimate relationship with them if you don't even know their name. In fact, the beginning of any relationship occurs through the introduction, which involves a revelation of names.

So we see that the two mainstream religions that claim to worship the same God are largely responsible for suppressing the Name of that God from the world through their translations and traditions. These traditions go against the entire emphasis of the Scriptures that describe the revelation of YHWH and the salvation that comes through His Name to all of the earth. He seeks a people who will covenant with Him. In order to enter into a covenant relationship with someone,

---

²² There are also those who transliterate the Name as Yahweh and pronounce it as Yah-way. Although probably the most common and popular usage, it does not appear to be a consistent pronunciation when we consider how the Name is pronounced when imbedded in other names. For instance, the Hebrew name Matthew is pronounced Mattityahu. It means: "gift from YHWH." The "yahu" portion is intended to reference the "YHW" portion of the Name. We see this throughout the Hebrew language and therefore it seems best to be consistent with this pronounciation when the Name stands alone. This subject is discussed in greater detail in the Walk in the Light series book entitled *Names*.

you must know their name.

This is no small issue. YHWH revealed Himself with a unique Name in a specific language. He desires for that Name to be known and we are either part of the problem or part of the solution. In fact, the first words spoken by YHWH at Mount Sinai were: "*I am YHWH your Elohim . . .*" This was the first Commandment of the Ten Commandments - not an issue to take lightly. Notice that YHWH refers to Himself as Elohim - not God.[23]

His Name is so important that in the Third Commandment He provides: "*You shall not take the Name of YHWH your Elohim in vain, for YHWH will not hold him guiltless who takes His Name in vain.*" (Exodus 20:7).

The word translated as "vain" in English is "shaw" (שוא) in Hebrew. It means "desolate or destroy." Therefore, the purpose of the Commandment is so that the Name of YHWH would not become "naught," which is exactly what has happened through the texts and the religions that are supposed to represent Him.[24]

This is abundantly evident in what is considered to be the most important Commandment, known as The Shema. It is found in Deuteronomy 6:4 and those in Judaism would recite it as follows: "*Hear O Yisrael Adonai your Elohim Adonai is One.*" A Christian would likely recite it as follows: "*Hear O Israel the LORD your God the LORD is one.*" In both instances, a passage intended to exalt and proclaim the Name of YHWH is

---

[23] The word God is an English word with Teutonic origins. It has been used to refer to pagan gods and the better word to use when referring to YHWH is Elohim. This subject is discussed further in the Walk in the Light series book entitled *Names*.

[24] When confronted with this truth, many religious individuals ignore it and choose instead to follow their own tradition. This is a serious mistake and reveals the heart of the individual. They call those who desire to properly exalt the Name as "legalistic" and indicate that this is not an important issue. Nothing could be further from the truth. Someday we will all stand before Him and give an account for what we did with His Name. There is actually a special Scroll of remembrance that was written "*for those who fear YHWH and meditate on His Name.*" (Malachi 3:16).

altered, and the Name is replaced with a title.

Now back to the text of Deuteronomy 31:24-26 and one final translation issue found in that passage. The English translation actually omits a word that is found 3 times in the Hebrew text. That missing word is known as the Aleph Taw (את) spelled with two Hebrew characters – "aleph" (א) and "taw" (ת). The "aleph" (א) is the first letter in the Hebrew alphabet and the "taw" (ת) is the last letter in the Hebrew alphabet. Essentially, this one word encompasses all of the words in Hebrew and it is never translated in English Bibles.[25]

When viewed in ancient Hebrew, we see that the aleph (𐤀) is shown as the head of an ox or a bull, signifying strength. The taw (X) is shown as an x, signifying a sign, mark or covenant. So the Aleph Taw (X𐤀), pronounced "et", literally means: "strength of the Covenant," "mark of the Covenant" or "sign of the Covenant."

It is a great mystery and it has incredible Messianic significance. Sadly, it is simply absent from all English translations of the Bible, but it is a really big deal. In fact, the Messiah Himself revealed Himself to be the Aleph Taw (את) in the Book of Revelation but, because the source texts used are written in Greek we read Alpha (A) and Omega (Ω) instead of Aleph Taw (את).[26] The absence of the Aleph Taw (את) in the English text results in English readers failing to see the

---

[25] In ancient understanding the Aleph Taw (את) was known as the "Memra" also known as "The Word." In modern Hebrew the "et" has been assigned the role as pointer to the direct object, but it is not consistently used throughout the Scriptures and typically provides insight into the Messiah.

[26] The Greek "alpha" (A) is the equivalent of the Hebrew "aleph" (א) and the Greek "omega" (Ω) is the same as the Hebrew "taw" (ת). The Messiah was a Hebrew speaking Yisraelite conversing with a Hebrew speaking disciple. So the Greek Alpha and Omega (AΩ) is clearly referring to the Aleph Taw (את). The subject of the Aleph Taw (את) is discussed and highlighted in the Walk in the Light Series book entitled *The Messiah*.

Messiah as the Word in the Old Testament.[27]

Finally, for the purposes of this discussion, "the Book of the Law" should be translated as "the Scroll of the Torah." So we should use the Hebrew word "Torah" (תורה) instead of "Law." This is a very important distinction and it is a grievous mistake to replace the word Torah with the word "Law." The word Torah has a very special meaning in the Scriptures.

The word Torah (תורה) in Hebrew means *"utterance, teaching, instruction or revelation from Elohim."* It comes from "horah" (הורה) which means *"to direct, to teach"* and derives from the stem "yara" (ירה) which means *"to shoot or throw."* Therefore there are two aspects to the word Torah: 1) aiming or pointing in the right direction, and 2) movement in that direction. This gives a much different sense than the word "Law." Following Torah involves walking "the straight and narrow path." It involves living righteously and avoiding sin.

In fact, the Hebrew word for sin is "cha-ta" (חטא). It means to miss the target and it is the opposite of the Torah. Torah points to the righteous straight path, but when we deviate from that path, we miss the mark and we sin. These are very basic concepts revealed through the Scriptures and easy to discern when examined in the original Hebrew language.

When showing the spelling of certain Hebrew words thus far, we mostly have viewed the modern Hebrew characters, although it is important to point out that the modern Hebrew language consists of a character set which is vastly different from the original language.

Just as we examined the Aleph Taw (𐤀𐤕) in ancient Hebrew, it is always valuable to look past the

---

[27] This is the mystery revealed in John 1 which states that "in the beginning was the Word." The Aleph Taw (את) is actually found two times in Genesis 1:1 and is intimately connected with Creation. Sadly, most English readers fail to make this connection because they never see the Aleph Taw (את) in the Hebrew text.

modern Hebrew to discern the original meaning of Hebrew characters and words. The modern Hebrew language uses characters that were developed around the 6th century BCE. The newer character set was likely adopted by the house of Judah during their Babylonian exile.

The language that was originally written and spoken by Hebrews is now referred to as Ancient Hebrew or Paleo-Hebrew. Although it went through a number of changes over the centuries, we are able to discern the original symbols and unlike modern Hebrew, these early Semitic languages used pictographs which actually resemble their meanings.

In modern Hebrew, the word Torah is spelled תורה and in the most Ancient Hebrew script it might look something like this: ΨϘΐX. When these ancient pictographic characters are joined together they result in a word whose meaning derives from combining the symbols. I find it particularly interesting in my research and studies to look at the original symbols of a word to derive its meaning.

The word Torah is a combination of four symbols:

- X - a X or a cross which means "a mark, seal or covenant."
- ΐ - a nail or peg which means "to add or secure."
- Ϙ - a head which means "a man, the head or the highest."
- Ψ - a person with hands raised which means "to reveal or behold."

Combining the meanings of these symbols gives us a profound definition of the word "Torah" as "behold the man nailed to the cross" or "behold the man who secures the covenant" or other similar derivations. From this word we see that the instructions, the Torah, secure mankind to the Covenant. How incredible that the Messiah is actually the strength of the Covenant and the One that seals the Covenant.

It should now be evident that the word "Law" is an inadequate and incorrect translation of the word Torah. The word Torah is more accurately defined as:

"the <u>instructions</u> of Elohim for His set apart people as was given through Mosheh and revealed by the life, death and resurrection of the Messiah."

The Torah contains instructions, guidance, and direction for those who desire to live righteous, set apart lives, in accordance with the will of Elohim. While these instructions were written on a scroll by Mosheh, they ultimately were intended to be inside of us.[28] That would be accomplished through the circumcision of our hearts, represented by the sign of the covenant – the circumcision of the flesh. YHWH gave the sign of circumcision to demonstrate the intimate relationship that He had planned for His Covenant people. He wants His Word to penetrate into our hearts so that we can love Him and serve Him with all our heart and with all our soul.

Here are a couple of Scripture passages that reveal this point.

"[12] And now, Yisrael, what does YHWH your Elohim require

---

[28] "[18] Therefore you shall lay up these words of mine in your heart and in your soul, and bind them as a sign on your hand, and they shall be as frontlets between your eyes. [19] You shall teach them to your children, speaking of them when you sit in your house, when you walk by the way, when you lie down, and when you rise up. [20] And you shall write them on the doorposts of your house and on your gates, [21] that your days and the days of your children may be multiplied in the land of which YHWH swore to your fathers to give them, like the days of the heavens above the earth." Deuteronomy 11:18-21

of you, but to fear YHWH your Elohim, to walk in all His ways and to love Him, to serve YHWH your Elohim with all your heart and with all your soul, ¹³ and to keep the Commandments of YHWH and His statutes which I command you today <u>for your good</u>? ¹⁴ Indeed heaven and the highest heavens belong to YHWH your Elohim, also the earth with all that is in it. ¹⁵ YHWH delighted only in your fathers, to love them; and He chose their descendants after them, you above all peoples, as it is this day. ¹⁶ Therefore circumcise the foreskin of your heart, and be stiff-necked no longer."
Deuteronomy 10:12-16

"And YHWH your Elohim will circumcise your heart and the heart of your descendants, to love YHWH your Elohim with all your heart and with all your soul, that you may live."
Deuteronomy 30:6

     YHWH gave His Bride Yisrael the Torah for her good. He was teaching His Bride Yisrael that true love must start from within, but it is demonstrated outwardly by our actions. YHWH explained to Yisrael that she could express her love and devotion through her obedience. So the Torah is literally at the heart of a love story between Elohim and His people.

     The word "instruction" clearly has a much different connotation than the word "Law." Parents instruct their children and guide their paths to keep them safe so that they can grow up healthy and blessed. While they clearly have rules for their household, those rules are administered in love.

     Of course, anyone who is married probably took a vow and likely promised to love, honor, cherish, and obey their spouse. This is the pattern for the relationship between YHWH and His people. While marriage may feel like bondage to some, when it is done right there is true love, blessing, peace, and contentment.

A healthy marriage can only occur when both parties submit their own wills and desires to the covenant – the joint venture and unified interests agreed upon between the two individuals. From that joining of two, we then see the fruit of children and a family. We are all given this real, intimate personal example of how YHWH desires to connect with His Bride, but the relationship must occur within the framework of the Torah which contains the terms or vows of the marriage covenant.[29]

Now governments and man-made institutions create laws that must be obeyed under threat of punishment. Those who disobey the laws of man are subject to consequences such as fines, imprisonment, and even death. Some societies are humane and fair in their implementation of their laws while others are cruel and despotic. Therefore, whatever experience a person has had with man-made laws - along with the sense of justice that they perceive from those laws – it will likely be carried over to their view of "the Law" in the Scriptures.

It is the use of the vague word "Law" instead of the specific word "Torah" that creates the problem alluded to at the beginning of this chapter. When people read about the "Law of God," they immediately attribute certain perceptions and emotions to the concept based upon their experiences with the "law of man."

This is particularly distressing since the word Torah is rendered in both the Septuagint (LXX), which is the Greek translation of the Hebrew Scriptures, and the Greek manuscripts of the New Testament using the word "nomos" (νομοσ). The Greek word "nomos" (νομοσ) specifically refers to the Torah and maintains

---

[29] In traditional Hebrew wedding covenant ceremonies there would be a "ketubah" or "writing" containing the terms of the covenant. It would have been a very natural thing for Yisrael to understand the Torah in that context. It defined and established boundaries for their relationship with YHWH.

the same sense of "instruction." Regrettably, when it is translated into English as "law," it loses that meaning.

Thus we see that both the Hebrew and the Greek words that refer to the "instructions of the Almighty" have been consistently and erroneously rendered as "Law" in the English translations of the Bible.

The Torah was given through the servant Moses at the wedding ceremony that occurred between YHWH and His Bride Yisrael at Mount Sinai. It was the marriage contract and it defined the terms of their relationship. YHWH made it very clear that He is "holy" and His Bride must also be "holy."[30] The prescribed conduct was set forth in the Torah as a wedding gift – the gift of righteousness.

It actually contained the keys to happiness, success, and prosperity. As long as Yisrael obeyed, she would share fellowship with her Husband and they could dwell together. Sadly, in the midst of the wedding process, Yisrael committed adultery by worshipping the golden calf. Idolatry is the same thing as adultery in the eyes of YHWH. When we worship other gods or participate in pagan practices, we are defiling ourselves and acting unfaithful toward him.

This results in separation and curses as we saw from the beginning in the Garden of Eden. So the Torah was a roadmap to life, given by a loving Elohim to a people who chose to enter into Covenant with Him. It pointed the way to blessings and warned of the curses associated with disobedience. YHWH made the curses particularly terrible to insure that His Bride would walk

---

[30] The word "holy" often seems mystical, but in the Hebrew language it simply means: "set apart." The Hebrew word is "qadosh" (קדש). So being "holy" or "qadosh" involves following the instructions found in the Torah that reveal the righteous path. When we are following the righteous instructions we are set apart – holy. Man was created in the image of Elohim and was meant to be holy as Elohim is holy (see Leviticus 21:8). That is why the Apostle Peter stated: "[15] but as He who called you is holy, you also be holy in all your conduct, [16] because it is written, "Be holy, for I am holy." 1 Peter 1:15-16.

the straight and narrow path. Sadly, even after the golden calf incident and the renewal of the Covenant, Yisrael repeatedly disobeyed.

This leads to a common misperception that the Torah was a burden - impossible to obey. That is a lie straight from the pit of hell intended to deceive people and lead them away from the Torah. If that were true, it would mean that YHWH is a cruel and abusive spouse, and nothing could be further from the truth. YHWH is the one who liberates and frees His Bride from bondage and slavery.

In fact, immediately prior to Yisrael entering into the Covenant, Moses specifically stated: *"For this Commandment which I command you today is not too difficult for you, nor is it out of reach."* (Deuteronomy 30:11 NASB). The Torah is very easy to understand. It provides instructions for how to treat one another and how to approach and worship YHWH.

The Torah was always looked upon as a gift from a loving Husband to a grateful Bride. It is a wonderful blessing to be cherished. Indeed, the longest and arguably the most incredible Psalm in the Scriptures is Psalm 119, which extolls both the Torah and the Hebrew language. If you read it in English you will miss most of the richness, beauty, and perfection but you can still get the point.[31]

Sadly, Christianity has missed the point, and the mark for that matter. The Christian religion refers to the instructions as "the Law" and, as previously mentioned, "the Law" makes us think of the myriad of rules and regulations imposed upon people by society to control

---

[31] Psalm 119 consists of 176 verses. It is divided into 22 sections based upon the number of characters in the Hebrew language. Each verse in each section begins with the corresponding letter in the Hebrew alphabet. In other words, the first eight verses all begin with "aleph" (א). The second set of eight verses all begin with "bet" (ב). The third set of eight verses all begin with "gimmel" (ג) and so on through "taw" (ת). It is a literal masterpiece and the focus is crystal clear – the Torah.

them, tax them and ultimately punish them if they disobey. Laws can be a blessing when properly and fairly administered, but the tendency is for them to become oppressive and repressive. We also know that religions can enslave and entangle people in their manmade rules, regulations and traditions.

That is exactly the impression I was given concerning the Torah, described to me as the Law. I was taught that the Law given to Yisrael was oppressive, that it was a curse, and that trying to obey it would put one under bondage. It is as if the Creator was trying to play some cruel joke upon Yisrael. This is the paradigm that most Christians inherit. That is why many perceive the Torah as bondage because, to them, it is impossible to obey.

In fact, a typical Christian retort to the suggestion that they should obey the Commandments is that "we can't keep the Law." That statement is born out of bad doctrine and ignorance, and is in direct contravention to the Scriptures.[32] We already saw that Moses said it was not too difficult. Are they calling Moses a liar? How about John then?

> "For this is the love of Elohim, that we keep His Commandments.
> And His Commandments are not burdensome."
> 1 John 5:3

---

[32] Nowhere in the Scriptures does it ever say that we cannot keep the Torah. Those who advocate such a position typically point to the fact that there is no Temple, so we cannot offer the sacrifices prescribed by the Torah. The simple fact is that there were times in history that there was no standing Tabernacle or Temple. That does not mean that the Torah failed to exist. Look at David. He was a righteous King who sought to build a house for YHWH after the Philistines destroyed the Mishkan and disrupted the worship of YHWH at Shiloh. David loved the Torah and obeyed the Torah even though he never saw the Temple completed by His son Solomon. After the Temple was destroyed by the Babylonians the exiles later returned and rebuilt the Temple. The Torah was not abolished during that period of exile. The same holds true after the destruction of the Temple by the Romans. The Torah was not abolished and Messiah will return to permanemtly restore and rebuild the Temple. I can assure you that the Torah will be the rule of His Kingdom.

Moses and John said the same thing. I sure hope that their credibility would be enough to dispel the erroneous notion that the Commandments are burdensome or too difficult to obey. Understanding this truth is critical to knowing Elohim.

So who ever said that we cannot or should not keep the Commandments? To answer that question all we need to do is look back to the Garden. The serpent lied to the woman and pegged Elohim as a liar. He insinuated that Elohim was simply deceiving the man and the woman in order to withhold certain knowledge from them. The serpent is the enemy of your soul who seeks your destruction and does not want you to obey. He wants you to disobey so that you will be separated from Elohim and die.[33]

Disobedience leads to separation from Elohim, to curses, death and destruction. Obedience leads to a communion and relationship with Elohim, to blessings, life and freedom. The relationship between Elohim and mankind was severed in the Garden, when the man and the woman chose to disobey.

Yisrael was given the opportunity to restore the breach that started in the Garden. They were encouraged to choose life![34] They were delivered from slavery specifically so they could be free to worship YHWH. Pharaoh's refusal to let them go resulted in the

---

[33] Genesis 3:1-5
[34] "[15] See, I have set before you today life and good, death and evil, [16] in that I command you today to love YHWH your Elohim, to walk in His ways, and to keep His Commandments, His statutes, and His judgments, that you may live and multiply; and YHWH your Elohim will bless you in the land which you go to possess. [17] But if your heart turns away so that you do not hear, and are drawn away, and worship other gods and serve them, [18] I announce to you today that you shall surely perish; you shall not prolong your days in the land which you cross over the Jordan to go in and possess. [19] I call heaven and earth as witnesses today against you, that I have set before you life and death, blessing and cursing; therefore choose life, that both you and your descendants may live; [20] that you may love YHWH your Elohim, that you may obey His voice, and that you may cling to Him, for He is your life and the length of your days; and that you may dwell in the land which YHWH swore to your fathers, to Abraham, Isaac, and Jacob, to give them." (Deuteronomy 30:15-20)

destruction of Egypt and his demise.

Only when they were free could they truly obey the Torah. That is why James refers to the Torah as *"the perfect Torah of liberty."*[35] James was the undisputed head of the followers of Yahushua after the death and resurrection of the Messiah. These followers were not part of a separate religion called Christianity. They were Yisraelites who believed that Messiah renewed the Covenant with Yisrael through His life, death and resurrection. Here is what James had to say about obeying the Torah.

"[22] But be doers of the Word, and not hearers only, deceiving yourselves. [23] For if anyone is a hearer of the word and not a doer, he is like a man observing his natural face in a mirror; [24] for he observes himself, goes away, and immediately forgets what kind of man he was. [25] But he who looks into the perfect law (Torah) of liberty and continues in it, and is not a forgetful hearer but a doer of the work, this one will be blessed in what he does." James 1:22-25

Notice how he is repeatedly encouraging people to be doers of the word while at the same time is referring to it as the "Torah of liberty." Obeying the Commandments does not lead to bondage, but rather freedom from sin. Doing the Word results in righteous conduct, also referred to as "works."

The Psalms also link the Torah with liberty. *"[44] So shall I keep Your Torah continually, forever and ever. [45] And I will walk at liberty, for I seek Your precepts."* (Psalm 119:44-45) It looks as though this Psalmist didn't get the Christian memo that the Torah would be abolished by the Messiah in the future. Of course the Scriptures are clear that the Torah is forever.

Obviously, as we have seen, nothing could be further from the truth. The Christian religion advocates

---

[35] This is a corrected translation. Obviously, the typical English translation refers to the Law, but it should refer to the Torah.

an unscriptural representation of the Torah. They claim that the Messiah "abolished the law"[36] when, in fact, the Scriptures specifically and repeatedly indicate that the Torah is forever.[37]

At this point, it is necessary to look to the One that Christians claim to serve and obey to see what He taught concerning the Torah. In fact, the Scriptures actually reveal that the Torah is the revelation of the Messiah.[38]

---

[36] This understanding is taken from a misunderstood verse in Ephesians 2:15. Nevertheless, it is mindboggeling to even think such a thing but Christians will use one misunderstood statement from a letter from Paul to essentially throw out the Covenant and the entire plan of YHWH. This tendency to cling to Paul in order to reject the Torah is all too common in Christianity and will be discussed further in Chapter 5.

[37] "The secret things belong to YHWH our Elohim, but those things which are revealed belong to us and to our children forever, that we may do all the words of the Torah." Deuteronomy 29:29. There are too many individual verses to quote on this point, but the reader is encouraged to study the Torah with this new understanding and discern how the instructions were in the Garden and they will continue on into the New Jerusalem. The Torah is simply the standard of conduct for the Kingdom of Elohim.

[38] In a Messianic Psalm we read: "⁷ Behold, I come; In the roll of the scroll it is written of me. ⁸ I delight to do Your will, O my Elohim, and Your Torah is within my heart."

3

The Messiah

While various Christian denominations disagree on many things, there is one thing they certainly agree upon - that Jesus is the Christ. The problem is that many pagan religions throughout the world and throughout history believed in pagan christs - all born on December 25th. In fact, this is a trademark of Babylonian derived sun worship. Almost all sun worshipping pagan religions include christs who were born at the winter solstice, which in ancient days used to be December 25th.[39] The word "christ" derives from "christos" which means "anointed." The word "Messiah" is Hebrew and, likewise, it means "anointed."[40]

So the real question is this - What distinguishes and qualifies a christ to be The Messiah, The Annointed One promised in the Scriptures, as opposed to all of the pagan christs found throughout history? The answer to this question is assumed by most Christians, but rightly posited by sceptics and truthseekers alike. In fact, most Jews[41] do not believe that Jesus was the Messiah. They

---

[39] Due to the procession of the equinoxes, the winter solstice has "processed" to December 21.

[40] The English word "Messiah" comes from the Hebrew word "moshiach" which literally means "anointed". In the Scriptures it could refer to a King or a Priest. Both positions involved being anointed with oil. The Messiah is the One anticipated to merge those two positions together as the Melchizedek – the Righteous King.

[41] The word Jew can be used in different contexts. It traditionally referred to someone belonging to the tribe of Judah or the political kingdom of the house of Judah or even the land of Judea. It was later expanded to include those belonging to the religion of Judaisn, but it can also refer to someone with no religious beliefs based upon their

say he does not qualify so they view him as just another pagan christ.

This is an important issue that the Christian religion must contend with because the Jesus that is taught in Christianity is not the same Yahushua[42] Who was born into the Tribe of Judah, was the very Torah in the flesh, lived and taught the Commandments, Renewed the Covenant with the House of Yisrael and the House of Judah, died as the Lamb of Elohim on Passover, rose from the grave and then sent the Spirit on the Appointed Time of Shavuot.

You see, the Messiah described in the Bible was a Yisraelite whose Hebrew name was Yahushua. He instructed and empowered His followers to obey the Commandments, while the Jesus of Christianity purportedly did the exact opposite.

The Hebrew Name Yahushua (יהושע) actually means "YHWH saves" or "YHWH is salvation." "Yah" (יה) or "Yahu" (יהו) represents the short form of the Name of the Father and "yasha" (ישע) means "save."[43] This is why the Messiah is also referred to as the Savior. His purpose is to save the Covenant people. In fact, when Joseph was told what to name Him, this

---

ethnic identity. In this context it simple refers to a person who ascribes to the religion of Judaism.

[42] The Messiah was a Yisraelite from the Tribe of Judah (Yahudah). He had the same Hebrew Name as the Patriarch commonly called Joshua. The Hebrew Name is spelled with either 5 letters (יהושע) or 6 letters (יהושוע) and is pronounced Yahu-shua. It contains the short form of the Name of the Father (Yahu) and the Hebrew root word for salvation (yasha), which is where we get the name Hosea, the original name of Joshua son of Nun (Numbers 13:16). The Name of the Messiah points to His emphasis on salvation as described by the Messenger on the Book of Matthew. "*And she will bring forth a Son, and you shall call His name Yahushua, for He will save His people from their sins.*" (Matthew 1:21) Sadly, you will not find the correct Hebrew Name Yahushua in most Bibles because they are modern translations of Greek texts in which certain names were Hellenized and changed from their original. It is quite certain that the true Name of the Messiah was the same as that of Joshua, more accurately transliterated from Hebrew as Yahushua. For a more detailed discussion of the Name of the Messiah see the Walk in the Light series book entitled *Names*.

[43] As a result, Yahushua literally came in His Father's Name. (See John 5:43)

description was given as the meaning of His Name – "*He shall save His people from their sins.*"[44]

"His people" are those within the Covenant and their sins are defined by and through the Covenant. The terms of the Covenant are found in the Torah. Therefore, the entire life and ministry of Yahushua was a fulfillment of the patterns contained within the Torah, and you need to be in the Covenant in order to be saved.[45]

So the very focus of the salvation provided by the Messiah involves the Torah but, according to most Christians, Jesus did away with the Law by abolishing the Torah. They actually believe that Jesus lived a perfect life according to the Torah, and then destroyed the very definition of His perfection - as if the Torah is a bad thing. Indeed, the entire concept is an oxymoron, because this would involve the Torah in the flesh destroying Himself.

The true Savior would have never done such a thing since He was the very embodiment of the Word of Elohim – the Torah in the Flesh (John 1:14). He walked, taught and lived the Torah as an example for us all. We are supposed to "follow Him" and the example He set for how to obey the Commandments.

He taught the *truth*, shined as a *light*, and showed us the *way* to *life*. Of course these were all descriptions of the Torah.

"*For the Commandment is a lamp, and <u>the Torah a light</u>; reproofs of instruction are <u>the way of life</u>.*"

---

[44] See Matthew 1:21. Again, in an English Bible you will read the name Jesus, but that is simply a translation tradition. The real Name is Yahushua and it unequivocally reveals the purpose of the Messiah, which is to save the people of YHWH from their sins. By sending His Son, YHWH will fulfill His Covenant promise and save His people from their sins.

[45] For a more detailed discussion of the patterns and prophecies fulfilled by the Messiah see the Walk in the Light series book entitled *The Messiah*.

Proverbs 6:23

"Your righteousness is an everlasting righteousness, and Your Torah is truth."
Psalm 119:142

Sadly, through language variations and the traditions of men, Christianity has developed a fictional christ named Jesus who is very different from the actual Hebrew Messiah named Yahushua.[46] This is a difficult statement for many to accept due to deeply rooted and strongly held traditions that they have inherited.

Almost every English speaking Christian came into the faith calling on "the Name of the LORD" and "Jesus." Neither of these references are historically or Scripturally sound, but most people are reticent to correct their understanding and speech. They think that by doing so, they will somehow be abandoning their faith or their Savior. The English titles and names are deeply ingrained within most Christians and very near and dear to their hearts. As a result, it is hard to accept that some of the doctrines we all have been taught and believed throughout our lives are grounded in tradition and even lies.

The power of tradition is undeniable. Christians regularly participate in pagan derived holidays such as Christmas and Easter. Most fail to recognize that these holidays originate from Babylonian sun worship rituals and were erroneously adopted by the Christian religion. Sadly, even when confronted with the truth most refuse to give them up.[47] When

---

[46] A presentation of the actual life, teaching and purpose of the Messiah within a proper historical and Scriptural context is provided in the Walk in the Light series book entitled *The Messiah*.

[47] For a more detailed discussion of the pagan traditions that have infiltrated the Christian religion see the Walk in the Light series book entitled *Pagan*

people develop pleasant memories and emotional attachments with certain traditions they often would rather continue in a lie than give up their tradition to follow the truth.

Of course, we should expect to be subjected to much deception if we believe the prophets. The prophet Jeremiah foretold of a time when *"the Gentiles shall come to You from the ends of the earth and say, 'Surely our fathers have inherited lies, worthlessness and unprofitable things.'"* Jeremiah 16:19.

Those familiar with the Scriptures know that there is a deceiver who desires the worship of men.[48] Through lies and traditions, the serpent seeks to divert the worship of mankind away from the one true Elohim. He has been doing this ever since the Garden, when he called Elohim a liar. Through seduction and deceit, he led the woman and the man away from the Commandments.

He continues those same tactics to this day and has most of the world under a spell through various diversions and religions that steer mankind away from the truth. Despite this awareness, most Christians believe that they are somehow immune from deception. The Scriptures tell otherwise.[49]

Christians have indeed inherited many lies from their fathers as prophesied by Jeremiah. One of those inherited lies involves the name of the Messiah. It is important to understand that the name Jesus never existed in ancient times, nor was it ever spoken in the Hebrew, Aramaic or Greek languages that were prevalent at the time of Messiah's arrival over 2,000 years ago. The Messiah was not named Jesus, nor was anyone named Jesus at that time. The name

---

Holidays.
[48] See Isaiah 14: 12-15. Also, the words spoken to "the prince of Tyre" and "the King of Tyre" in Ezekiel 28 are thought by many to also apply to satan.
[49] Peter specifically warned that untaught people were twisting the Scriptures and the Letters of Paul to their own destruction. (See 2 Peter 3:15-16)

simply did not exist.

It was not until the English language developed that the name of Jesus was spoken, because there is no letter J in the languages spoken in ancient times.[50] In fact, the letter J is a fairly recent addition to linguistics, arriving only about 400 years ago.[51]

This is not simply about the spelling or pronunciation of a name though. In the Hebrew culture, names are very important and describe the essence of a person. The Hebrew name Yahushua is the same name as the one we call Joshua in English. We are supposed to make the connection between the Messiah and that Patriarch who brought the Covenant Assembly of Yisrael into the Promised Land. So, if you were to call the Messiah by an English name, at the very least, you should call Him Joshua - which means: "YHWH saves" or "YHWH is salvation."[52]

The Name defines the very purpose and function of the work of the Messiah. While Joshua, the

---

[50] The English language developed between the 14th century and the 17th century. Most agree that the letter J did not come into existence until the 1600's. Therefore, the name "Jesus" has only been in existence for about 400 years. Prior to that time the Greek name "Iesus" prevailed and it is apparent that the name "Iesus" was used to replace the true Hebrew Name Yahushua. This is a historically provable fact. There is no debate on this at all. When someone insists on calling the Messiah Jesus, it is because they have chosen a tradition over truth. I don't care how long they have called on this name, how much they revere this name or how deeply they think they were saved by this name - it was not the name of the Messiah described in the Scriptures. While they may have expressed faith in the One described in the Scriptures, it is critical that they correct their traditions according to the truth.

[51] The letter "J" derived from the letter "I" and originally carried the "Y" sound. It was not until the early 1600's that the letter was pronounced with the "jay" sound. So, to properly transliterate both the Names of the Messiah and the Patriarch, it should be pronounced Yahushua.

[52] Of course, the English Name Joshua is also incorrect because it contains a "J" but the English transliteration better connects to the original Hebrew Name that it is supposed to represent. The name Jesus is not connected to the Hebrew Name Yahushua at all in either a translated or transliterated sense. In any event, when we transition from one language to another, we are supposed to transliterate names so that they sound the same from language to language. Sadly, people who have been brought up with the tradition of calling the Messiah by a fictitious name cling to this tradition rather than adopt the truth.

servant of Moses, eventually led Yisrael into the Promised Land, likewise, the Messiah will fulfill that same pattern. As Yisrael crossed the Jordan from the Land of Moab into the Land of Canaan they were corporately "baptized" in the Jordan. They were then circumcised and proceeded to conquer and inhabit the Promised Covenant Land.

Through the baptism, death and resurrection of the Messiah, we can now be baptized in the Spirit and have our hearts circumcised. As a result, we can enter into the Promised Land, which represents a return to the Garden and the Kingdom of Elohim.

The Messiah came to fulfill these patterns and, in order to place His teachings and ministry into context, it is important to understand this connection. The name Jesus, on the other hand, derives from unknown or possibly pagan sun worship origins. It was not and is not the name of the Messiah. The name Iesus was inserted into Greek texts in place of the true Name.[53] That Greek name was later translated as Jesus in the English language.

Just because you have learned the wrong name, prayed to the wrong name, or even expressed your worship to the wrong name does not mean that He never heard you! He is patient with all of us as we seek His truth and walk in His ways. We all fall short and there is forgiveness when we repent. The question is whether we will repent and change our ways or stubbornly insist upon following our traditions – even when we know they are wrong. When we discover the truth, we need to give

---

[53] The name Iesus is connected with the name of a healing god and a child of Zeus, the Greek king of the gods. It is likely that converts to Christianity, many of whom came out of sun worship, replaced the name to identify Yahushua as the Son of God. This type of thing clearly occurred with the New Testament texts. For example, the name of the prophet Elijah is rendered as Helios in the Greek texts. Of course Helios is the name of the Greek god of the sun. It makes perfect sense that the same would be done with the "Son of God."

thanks, act upon it, and move on.

Another Christian tradition involves using the term "christ," which was a Greek title used to describe the Greek gods. Of course, all these Greek gods derived from sun worship that can be traced back to ancient Babylon.

So, a Greek name and title, both rooted in Babylonian sun worship, have been adopted by Christians to refer to the Hebrew Messiah. This mistake is more than simply a linguistic technicality. It has far-reaching theological implications.

If it does not matter what you call the Messiah, then Christians should just make the final leap into pagan sun worship and begin calling Him Tammuz, Dionysus, Bacchus, Mithra, Horus, Helios, etc. These, and many other pagan sun gods, were all declared to be born on December 25th. As a result, the Christian religion decided to use the same date, thus making it easier for pagans to convert to Christianity.[54] This causes great confusion, muddies the waters and dilutes the identity of the real Messiah and the Father.

Names are extremely important because they form the basis of any relationship. If you decide to worship a particular god you must identify that god by name. The name then reveals their function, their teaching and their prescribed method of worship.

We cannot have a real relationship with anyone, god or man, if we do not know their name. YHWH specifically identified Himself by Name and He gave very clear and specific instructions on how He desired to be served. He then sent His Son,

---

[54] There are many other sun gods who share the birth date of December 25th. The point is so obvious for anyone who looks at history but regardless most people enjoy the pagan celebration of Christmas, so they would rather continue to worship as the pagans worship.

Who carried the Name of the Father. It happened this way so that there would be no confusion about what He was teaching.

When Yahushua declared "*I and My Father are One,*" He meant it.[55] He was teaching people how to worship the Father exactly as YHWH had previously instructed Yisrael through Moses. Yisrael had broken the Covenant and strayed from the straight path like scattered and lost sheep. Yahushua came to renew the Covenant and shepherd the flock.

There was no difference between His teaching and the Father's instruction. Indeed, He was the very Word of the Father manifested in the flesh.

John specifically stated the following: "*[1] In the beginning was the Word, and the Word was with Elohim, and the Word was Elohim. [2] He was in the beginning with Elohim. [3] All things were made through Him, and without Him nothing was made that was made. [4] In Him was life, and the life was the light of men. [5] And the light shines in the darkness, and the darkness did not comprehend it.*" (John 1:1-5)

This is not some abstract notion, but a very real word seen only in the Hebrew text. Recall the Aleph Taw (את) that we discussed earlier. Well, the Aleph Taw (את) is actually located at the beginning of the Scriptures. It is located two times in the first verse of Genesis and it reveals clearly that the Messiah was indeed present at creation and an active participant in the Creation process.

That word, the Aleph Taw (את), was also affixed to the "light" described as good in Genesis.

"*[3] Then Elohim said, 'Let there be light' and there was

---

[55] John 10:30

> light. ⁴ And Elohim saw את-the light (את־האור), that it was good; and Elohim divided the light from the darkness."
> Genesis 1:3-4

That light was the first thing spoken and manifested into Creation on Day 1 and John confirmed that the Aleph Taw (את) was both the Word and the Light – the Messiah.[56]

Of course the Scriptures described the Word as "light." "*Your Word is a lamp to my feet and a light to my path.*" (Psalm 119:105) It lights our way so we can see the straight path and walk in it. The Word of YHWH is also His instructions in righteousness provided through His Commandments. "*My tongue shall speak of Your Word, for all Your Commandments are righteousness.*" (Psalm 119:172)

In order to know how to be righteous and live righteously, you must obey the Commandments. No less than 36 times in Psalm 119 is the "Word" compared to the "Torah" or the "Commandment." That is because the Word and the righteous Commandments are the same. In fact, Moses said "*I stood between YHWH and you at that time, to declare to you the Word of YHWH; for you were afraid because of the fire, and you did not go up the mountain.*" (Deuteronomy 5:5)

In this passage, in the Hebrew, when we read "the Word," we actually read "et-debar" (את־דבר). The Aleph Taw (את) is affixed to "the Word" (דבר), revealing the clear connection. Again, we do not see this in our English translations, but it is clearly seen in the Hebrew text. Therefore, those who believe in the Messiah and follow His teachings should be very interested in living and obeying the Commandments.

---

[56] The Messiah, as the Word, was the manifestation of YHWH in the physical realm. Both sound and light are frequencies.

So, the Word is an intimate and integral part of the Messiah, because He is the Word. He was and is the physical manifestation of YHWH in the physical realm. He is the form that YHWH chose to reveal Himself to us through sight and sound – in the flesh. As a result, His mission, when He came in the flesh, was to transmit the pure Word as YHWH had done from the Mountain and through Moses. He made that point abundantly clear.

*"I have manifested Your Name to the men whom You have given Me out of the world. They were Yours, You gave them to Me, and they have kept **Your Word**."*
John 17:6

"I have given them Your Word; and the world has hated them because they are not of the world, just as I am not of the world."
John 17:14

"Sanctify them by Your truth. Your Word is truth."
John 17:17

The purpose of the Messiah, as the Word in the flesh, was to point people in the right direction, back to the ancient and righteous path that Yisrael had strayed from. Indeed, the first recorded word spoken by the Messiah was "repent."[57]

"Repent" specifically means "turn back" or "return." The question everyone should ask is this, "Return to what?" Obviously, return to the Father, return to the Covenant, return to the relationship by living according to the instructions. It was really a very simple message, easily understood by the Yisraelites.

If this could not be any more obvious, during one

---
[57] Matthew 4:17

of His first recorded teachings, Messiah stated:

> "*17* Do not think that I came to destroy the Torah or the Prophets. I did not come to destroy but to fulfill. *18* For assuredly, I say to you, till heaven and earth pass away, one jot or one tittle will by no means pass from the law till all is fulfilled. *19* Whoever therefore breaks one of the least of these Commandments, and teaches men so, shall be called least in the kingdom of heaven; but whoever does and teaches them, he shall be called great in the kingdom of heaven. *20* For I say to you, that unless your righteousness exceeds the righteousness of the scribes and Pharisees, you will by no means enter the kingdom of heaven." (Matthew 5:17-20)

From this passage we understand that He was drawing a clear line between the Commandments and religious teachings not in line with the Commandments. He came to challenge the authority of religious men and their traditions rather than to abolish the Torah. In fact, as long as heaven and earth remain, not the smallest part of the Torah would pass away.[58] This is the exact opposite of what Christianity teaches. Most Christians believe that Jesus abolished the Torah, but Yahushua said He did not.

In fact, He always taught the Torah. Read His response when a Scribe asked which was the greatest Commandment.

> "*29* Yahushua answered him, 'The first of all the commandments is: Hear, O Yisrael, YHWH our Elohim, YHWH is one. *30* And

---

[58] See also Luke 16:17 where Messiah states "And it is easier for heaven and earth to pass away than for one tittle of the law to fail."

you shall love YHWH your Elohim with all your heart, with all your soul, with all your mind, and with all your strength. This is the first commandment. ³¹ And the second, like it, is this: You shall love your neighbor as yourself. There is no other commandment greater than these.' ³² So the scribe said to Him, 'Well said, Teacher. You have spoken the truth, for there is one Elohim, and there is no other but He. ³³ And to love Him with all the heart, with all the understanding, with all the soul, and with all the strength, and to love one's neighbor as oneself, is more than all the whole burnt offerings and sacrifices.' ³⁴ Now when Yahushua saw that he answered wisely, He said to him, 'You are not far from the kingdom of Elohim.'" (Mark 12:29-34)

In response to the question Yahushua would have declared in Hebrew "Shema Yisrael." Of course, He was quoting the greatest Commandment found in Deuteronomy 6:4-5, known as The Shema. The Hebrew word "shema" (שמע) means "hear and obey."

This word clearly reflects the difference between eastern and western thought. Western translators, who translate the text into English, simply insert the word "hear" which gives the reader the impression that we are supposed to listen. Listening is a fairly passive activity and is meaningless unless it results in some sort of action or behavior.

According to eastern thought, the word "shema" implies listening to the Commands and then obeying the Commands. It involves action, and that is how we demonstrate our love for Elohim. We listen to His instructions and we obey them.

Through this process we also love our neighbor

because He loves our neighbors. If we truly love Him then that must result in our loving others. Of course, that is actually a Commandment found in the Book of Leviticus.

"*17* *You shall not hate your brother in your heart. You shall surely rebuke your neighbor, and not bear sin because of him. 18 You shall not take vengeance, nor bear any grudge against the children of your people, but you shall love your neighbor as yourself: I am YHWH."* (Leviticus 19:17-18)

So Yahushua was not giving any new or different teaching, and He in no way gave the impression that the Torah would be abolished. He distilled the Torah down to its essence – the love of Elohim and the love of our neighbor. Notice also what He said to the Scribe – *"You are not far from the kingdom of Elohim."* In other words – he got it.

Now read a similar teaching resulting from a different question found in Luke 10. In that text, a Scribe asked Him what he must do to inherit eternal life. Now at this point, every Christian should be paying very close attention because salvation and eternal life is the ultimate goal of Christianity.

In response to the Scribe's question Yahushua asked a question: *"What is written in the Torah? What is your reading of it?"* According to His question, He is clearly suggesting that eternal life is found in the Torah. The Scribe responded as follows: *"You shall love YHWH your Elohim with all your heart, with all your soul, with all your strength, and with all your mind, and your neighbor as yourself."* Notice that his answer was the same as Yahushua had previously given. He quoted the Shema from Deuteronomy 6:5 and also Leviticus 19:18.

Yahushua's response was simple and to the point: *"You have answered rightly; do this and you will live."* So He affirmed that the way to eternal life was indeed found in the Torah.

Here is another passage dealing with eternal life.
"*¹⁷ Now as He was going out on the road, one came running, knelt before Him, and asked Him, 'Good Teacher, what shall I do that I may inherit eternal life?' ¹⁸ So Yahushua said to him, 'Why do you call Me good? No one is good but One, that is, Elohim. ¹⁹ You know the Commandments: Do not commit adultery, Do not murder, Do not steal, Do not bear false witness, Do not defraud, Honor your father and your mother.' ²⁰ And he answered and said to Him, 'Teacher, all these things I have kept from my youth.' ²¹ Then Yahushua, looking at him, loved him, and said to him, 'One thing you lack: Go your way, sell whatever you have and give to the poor, and you will have treasure in heaven; and come, take up the cross, and follow Me.' ²² But he was sad at this word, and went away sorrowful, for he had great possessions.*" (Matthew 10:17-22)

Notice that this time He mentioned some of the Ten Commandments. This is a very Hebrew way of referring to all of the Commandments, not just the ones mentioned. Again, He was not adding to the Commandments or taking away. He was simply telling the man to obey the Commandments.

Now Yahushua knew that the man had made his riches into an idol. While the man obeyed the Commandments, he had placed greater importance in his goods and possessions and was unable to give them up. Thus, he did not love Elohim *with all his heart, with all his soul, with all his mind, and with all his strength.*

The same teaching is found in Luke 18. Again, when Yahushua was asked how a person inherits eternal life, He pointed to the Commandments. "*You know the Commandments: Do not commit adultery, Do not murder, Do not steal, Do not bear false witness, Honor your father and your mother.*" (Luke 18:20)

Many people erroneously believe that Yahushua disobeyed the Commandments because that is what the religious leaders asserted.⁵⁹ There were many instances when Yahushua ignored the religious traditions concerning the Sabbath in order to show the true purpose of the Sabbath, but He never violated the Commandments.

We could go on and on and dissect all of the Gospels and I challenge you to do so. While you will find plenty of instances where Yahushua challenged and thwarted the traditions of the Pharisees, you will not find any instance where He disobeyed the Torah.

He always upheld the Commandmensts. He obeyed the Torah and He showed us how to do it by shifting the focus to love. He revealed that the Torah was all about showing us how to love YHWH and love our neighbor. If we can get that right then we will get into the Kingdom through Him.

The religious leaders had gone astray. They had taken the Torah and made it into a religion rather than a relationship. They were so caught up in their "do's and don'ts" that they had created just another religion to dictate people's lives and subject people to religious bondage.

Yahushua came with the authority of the Father to challenge the authority of the Scribes and Pharisees who had hijacked the Torah and put the sheep under their oppressive rules and regulation. He came to set the captives free and that is why the religious leaders hated Him and sought to kill Him.

Yahushua described them as lawless hypocrites. "²⁷ *Woe to you, Scribes and Pharisees, hypocrites! For you are like whitewashed tombs which indeed appear beautiful outwardly, but inside are full of dead men's bones and all uncleanness.* ²⁸ *Even so you also outwardly appear*

---

⁵⁹ See John 5:18

righteous to men, but inside you are full of hypocrisy and lawlessness." (Matthew 23:27-28)

While they appeared righteous on the outside because of their traditions and behaviors they were unclean on the inside. They were so concerned about the flesh that they forgot that their hearts needed to be circumcised.

Remember the greatest Commandment - The Shema. "⁴ Hear, O Yisrael: YHWH our Elohim, YHWH is one! ⁵ You shall love YHWH your Elohim with all your heart, with all your soul, and with all your strength. ⁶ And these words which I command you today shall be in your heart." (Deuteronomy 6:4-6)

The point was always that the Commandments should be inside of us, written on our hearts. The heart is the organ that pumps the blood and the life through the body. It also represents the seat of passion where our thoughts and actions are purposed.

Therefore, the Words in our hearts become alive as we live them out in all dimensions.[60] As those written words get inside of us they become alive through our thoughts, speech and actions. Only when the Word is inside us can we truly live righteous and sinless lives. This is clearly set forth in the Scriptures.

> "¹⁰ With my whole heart I have sought You;
> Oh, let me not wander from Your Commandments!
> ¹¹ Your word I have hidden in my heart,
> that I might not sin against You."
> Psalm 119:10-11

---

[60] This was the Renewed Covenant prophesied by the Prophet Jeremiah. "But this is the covenant that I will make with the את-house of Israel after those days, says YHWH: I will put My את-Torah in their minds, and write it on their hearts; and I will be their Elohim, and they shall be My people." Jeremiah 31:33. Incredibly, the Aleph Taw (את) is affixed to the House of Yisrael and the Torah. This reveals that the Messiah would be the One to renew the Covenant and write the Torah on our

The Pharisees had a form of godliness, but they did not have the Words inside them. They were dirty on the inside and needed to be washed by the water of the Word.[61]

"²⁵ Woe to you, scribes and Pharisees, hypocrites! For you cleanse the outside of the cup and dish, but inside they are full of extortion and self-indulgence. ²⁶ Blind Pharisee, first cleanse the inside of the cup and dish, that the outside of them may be clean also." (Matthew 23:25-26)

According to Yahushua, the Pharisees were not getting into the Kingdom. "For I say to you, that unless your righteousness exceeds the righteousness of the scribes and Pharisees, you will by no means enter the kingdom of heaven." (Matthew 5:20) The Pharisees were more concerned with their man-made rules, laws and traditions than they were the Commandments of Elohim. Yahushua made this clear when He said: "All too well you reject the Commandment of Elohim, that you may keep your tradition." (Mark 7:9)

Yahushua was the anointed King and, as such, He could determine who gets into the Kingdom. In His role as both King and Priest He renewed the Covenant through His broken body and shed blood.[62]

It is a free gift afforded to everyone. We cannot earn that gift. The question then is - What do we do with that gift? Once we have been made clean by the blood of the Lamb, do we continue to walk in the filth of disobedience or do we walk in the light of His Commandments?

Yahushua gave a clear and unequivocal answer. He said: "If you love Me, <u>keep</u> My Commands." (John 14:15) This was the same instruction given to Adam and Yisrael. The word translated as "keep" is "shamar" (שמר) in Hebrew. Again, it means to "watch, guard and

---

[61] Ephesians 5:26
[62] See Matthew 26:28, Mark 14:24, Luke 22:20 and Hebrews 9:20

protect."

The night before His crucifixion, Yahushua participated in the Covenant meal of the Passover. It was during this meal that He began the renewal of the Covenant with Yisrael as the High Priest according to the Order of Melchizedek.[63]

He stated that the bread represented His body and the wine represented His blood.[64] His presence at the Passover meal represented the Passover Lamb – the Lamb of Elohim. Later, on Passover Day, His body would be broken and His blood would be shed just as had been symbolically done with the bread and the wine at the Passover meal.[65]

How interesting that there were 12 disciples at that Covenant meal, representing the 12 tribes of Yisrael. One of them left before the meal was completed. His name was Judas, which means Judah, or rather Yahudah. It was during this Appointed Time that the Covenant was renewed.[66]

It was not a brand new Covenant, but rather the long anticipated renewal promised by the prophets. The renewal would be with the House of Yisrael and the House of Yahudah.[67] There is no Covenant prophesied with an entity called the Church. Rather, it was the Covenant promised by the Prophet Jeremiah that would be renewed.[68]

---

[63] See Genesis 14:18, Psalm 110:1-4, Hebrews 5-7
[64] Matthew 26:26-29, Mark 14:22-25, Luke 22:19-22
[65] It is important to realize that a Scriptural day begins in the evening, after sunset. The Passover meal begins at the beginning of Day 14 in Month 1, right at sunset – between the evenings. Therefore, Yahushua was crucified on Passover Day and placed in the Tomb before the High Sabbath of the Feast of Unleavened Bread.
[66] Passover is a special Appointed Time detailed in the Scriptures. Yahushua fulfilled the Appointed Times as part of His work and will further fulfill them in the future when He returns. For more information regarding the Scriptural Appointed Times see the Walk in the Light series book entitled *Appointed Times*.
[67] Jeremiah 31:31-34
[68] For a detailed discussion of the Scriptural Covenants see the Walk in the Light series book entitled *Covenants*.

> *"But this is the Covenant that I will make with the את-House of Yisrael after those days, says YHWH: I will put My את-Torah in their minds, and write it on their hearts; and I will be their Elohim, and they shall be My people."*
> Jeremiah 31:33

This is critical to understand because your future depends upon your relationship with YHWH and His Son. That relationship is defined by a Covenant. You must determine whether or not you are in that Covenant before it is too late. Many will, in fact, be deceived and will be rejected by the Messiah. They will think that they are in a relationship with the Son, but they will be wrong.

Here is a very chilling statement made by Yahushua. "*²¹ Not everyone who says to Me, Lord, Lord, shall enter the Kingdom of Heaven, but he who does the will of My Father in heaven. ²² Many will say to Me in that day, 'Lord, Lord, have we not prophesied in Your name, cast out demons in Your name, and done many wonders in Your name?' ²³ And then I will declare to them, 'I never knew you; depart from Me, you who practice lawlessness!'*" (Matthew 7:21-23)

Notice that there will be <u>many</u> people calling Him "Lord." They think that they are following Him and doing His will but they are actually deceived. He does not know them, which means He does not have a relationship with them. They may be running around doing all sorts of seemingly religious activities, but they are not in Covenant with Him. He actually defines them by their actions - they are "lawless." The Greek word is "anomia" (ἀνομία), which specifically means "without the Torah."

Only those who do "the will of the Father" will enter into the Kingdom and "the will of the Father" is expressed through the Commandments. The Christian religion is notorious for rejecting the Torah and claiming their "liberty" through "grace." They misunderstand both the Torah and grace, and the writings of Paul are often used to justify a rejection of the Torah because of that grace.[69]

Those who subscribe to such false teachings do so to their own destruction. They should expect to be sent away by Yahushua through His clear and unequivocal words. He shed His blood so that you can be forgiven, cleansed and restored to the Renewed Covenant. If you reject the very Covenant that was offered to you by grace, then your fate is certain.

Yahushua clearly stated who would inherit the kingdom – "the poor in spirit."[70] "To be poor in spirit means to have emptied yourself of all desire to exercise personal self-will, and, what is just as important, to have renounced all preconceived opinions in the wholehearted search for [Elohim]. It means to be willing to set aside your present habits of thought, your present views and prejudices, your present way of life if necessary; to jettison, in fact, anything and everything that can stand in the way of your finding [Elohim]."[71] This includes any inherited customs and traditions that do not conform to the Scriptures.

There is a wedding feast being prepared by the Messiah and all are invited. You must make yourself ready and come on His terms, not your own terms. Those who refuse to do it His way will find themselves cast into outer darkness where there will be weeping and gnashing of teeth.[72]

As it turns out, the Christian "christ,"

---

[69] The relationship between the Torah and grace is examined in detail in the Walk in the Light series book entitled *The Law and Grace*.
[70] Matthew 5:3
[71] *The Sermon on the Mount, The Key to Success in Life*, Emmet Fox, Grosset & Dunlap (1938) page 22.
[72] Matthew 22:1-14

represented through Christian tradition, is in many ways diametrically opposed to the true Messiah described in the Scriptures.

We have the clear words and teachings of Yahushua in the texts that are often ignored or twisted to fit the lawless paradigm created by Christianity. As a result, the Jesus of Christianity has morphed into a sort of anti-christ or anti-messiah.[73] The Christian religion has attempted to replace the Torah teaching Yahushua with a Law abolishing Jesus.[74]

Of course this should be no surprise because the one described as "antichrist" or rather "anti-messiah" in First and Second John is not simply opposed to the Messiah. He seeks to replace the Messiah and receive the worship, the throne and the authority that belongs to Yahushua.

Paul referred to this individual as "the lawless one" (2 Thessalonians 2:8) and the hallmark of this lawless one will be his opposition to the Torah.

So, if Christians believe that their christ abolished the Torah, then they worship an "antichrist." These are hard words and this is a hard truth. Many have difficulty accepting them, but there is no gentle way of presenting these facts. The enemy seeks to deceive the elect through false christs and false prophets. This was clearly foretold by Yahushua.

"For false christs and false prophets will rise and show signs

---

[73] This seems impossible for most Christians to comprehend, but this is critical to understand. Again, Yahushua specifically warned of such an event. *"For false christs and false prophets will rise and show great signs and wonders to deceive, if possible, even the elect."* Matthew 24:24. See also Mark 13:22. The Hebrew Messiah was the living Torah. He did not come to abolish the Torah, a thing commonly attributed to the Christian Jesus.

[74] This is often a difficult concept for Christians to grasp. Of course, a paradigm shift is never easy, but this one is critical. You must understand that the Jesus espoused by Christianity does not accurately represent the Messiah Yahushua. You must determine who you follow and that is demonstrated by how you live.

> *and wonders to deceive, if possible, even the elect."*
> Matthew 24:2, Mark 13:22

What better way to deceive the elect than to hijack the identity of the One he opposes and hates. As a result of this deception, most Christians believe that the Commandments are no longer applicable to the people of Elohim. This is why they have no Scriptural definition of sin and this is why they fail to point converts to the Covenant path.

They erroneously equate "obedience" with "legalism," as if obeying the Commandments was something repulsive and to be avoided. This is only a problem if you think that you can earn your salvation through obedience. You cannot work your way into the Kingdom, but your works will definitely determine your place in the Kingdom.[75]

The only way to get into the Kingdom is to pass through the door covered by the blood of the Lamb. This is why Passover is the first Appointed Time in the yearly cycle of special times that we are commanded to observe.

It reveals that the way into the Covenant relationship is by the shed blood of the Lamb of Elohim. The key is that you must walk through the door into the Covenant within which the blood was shed – not some other door, religion or covenant. Obedience is simply our loving response to the free gift of atonement provided to us through that shed blood.

Yahushua came according to the Covenant promises to prepare a people who will truly love and serve Elohim - a people who will be His Bride. That is why His true disciples repent and are then baptized in

---

[75] "Whoever therefore breaks (relaxes) one of the least of these Commandments, and teaches men so, shall be called least in the kingdom of heaven; but whoever does and teaches them, he shall be called great in the kingdom of heaven." Matthew 5:19

His Name. By doing so, they acknowledge His authority to forgive us and wash us clean from our sins.

This is all plainly stated in the Scriptures, yet many fail to recognize or accept this truth. The reason for this is generally attributed to the writings of Paul.

4

But Paul Said . . .

It is interesting to see the reaction of most Christians when they are told that in order to have a relationship with Elohim they must actually do what He says and do what His Son says. In other words, they must obey the Commandments. We are simply talking about obedience, but you might think that you were handling a deadly disease.

The typical response is to withdraw with disdain and horror, and the typical retort is to recite a quote from one of the letters attributed to Paul. Most Christians use the writings of Paul as a justification for disobeying the Torah. Their logic is that since the writings of Paul are found in the Bible then those letters must be the Word of God, and since they are in the New Testament then they must supersede the words in the Old Testament.

Of course, this logic is flawed on many levels. First of all, inclusion in the Bible does not automatically make something "the Word of Elohim." We know very clearly when something is the Word of Elohim or the word of a man because the text indicates who is speaking the word. Sometimes the Scriptures merely contain history and even satan is quoted in the Scriptures.[76]

There are plenty of critics of Paul and it is not my desire to attack this individual. In fact, I have spent considerable time in my other books analyzing the writings of Paul and even defending, explaining or

---

[76] See Job 1 and 2. Also, satan is quoted in the Gospel of Matthew in Chapter 4 and the Gospel of Luke at Chapter 4.

justifying his intentions.[77] This defense may or may not be warranted depending upon your opinion of Paul.

For the purposes of this discussion I do not desire to justify or attack him. It is appropriate to have a brief and frank analysis of the matter because Paul plays such an important role in popular Christian thought.

The writings of Paul found in the Bible consist of different letters of instruction that he wrote to certain people or assemblies concerning a variety of issues – some doctrinal, some administrative and some personal in nature. Those letters are by no means a thorough and comprehensive review of the Torah.

At most, they are midrashic[78] studies and interpretations concerning specific issues. At the least, they are mere opinions. Never can they be considered "the word of Elohim" and even Paul himself would not have considered them to be Scriptures. In his time, the Scriptures were defined as the Torah, the Prophets and the Writings. These are the texts that he would have considered to be the Scriptures, not his own letters.[79]

I know of no instance when he proclaimed that "the Word of Elohim came to me and said . . ." or "YHWH spoke to me and declared . . ." These are the hallmarks of the Word of Elohim that we find throughout the Scriptures and, of course, we have quotes from the Messiah – the actual Word of Elohim in the flesh.

No one is supposed to add or subtract from the Torah and that is why Yahushua came against the

---

[77] See the Walk in the Light series published by Shema Yisrael Publications. This may be rooted in my Christian upbringing that the Bible is the inerrant word of Elohim so there is a natural tendency to defend everything contained in the Bible.

[78] "Midrash" (מדרש) is a Hebrew word that is used when referring to the study and interpretation of Scriptural texts. It involves filling in gaps and resolving problems in the interpretation of difficult passages. So at most, the letters of Paul would involve the explaining of difficult Torah passages and teaching the Torah. He could never be permitted or authorized to change the Torah through his letters.

[79] See Romans 15:4 and 1 Corinthians 15:3-4

Pharisees. They were changing the Torah by adding to and subtracting from it. With that precedent we must understand that there is no way that Paul had any authority to add to or subtract from the Torah.

Again, the Scriptures in his day were clear and established – The Torah, the Prophets and the Writings. Paul professed to believe the Torah and the Prophets.[80] In fact, it was his practice to use the Scriptures to show that Yahushua was the Messiah.[81]

Hundreds of years after his death, the Christian religion decided to add Paul's letters to a new canon of texts referred to as the New Testament. These texts were then considered to be Scriptures and, as a result, many Christians make the leap and declare that those letters are the Word of God. They then use those words to nullify the original Scriptures and advocate lawlessness. This is really quite amazing when you think about it, but they do so because they have been taught that the entire Bible was compiled by the Holy Spirit, and therefore every word of the Bible constitutes the inerrant Word of God.

Of course, history is clear that the compilation of the Bible was a process largely conducted by the Roman Empire and the official state religion – the Roman Catholic Church.[82] There is no way to prove whether or not the Bible contains all texts specifically inspired by the Holy Spirit or all the Words spoken by Elohim. In fact, to this day various Christian sects and denominations include different texts in their Bibles.

One thing is certain, all of the letters in the Bible, known as Epistles, were letters written by men to other individuals or assemblies. They provide advice and guidance, but they do not claim to be prophetic words

---

[80] Acts 24:14 and Acts 26:22
[81] Acts 18:28 and Acts 28:23
[82] For a detailed discussion on the compilation of the Bible see the Walk in the Light series book entitled *The Scriptures*.

directly from Elohim.

So to quote a letter from Paul and claim that it is the Word of God is not accurate and leads to problems. These letters of Paul were written to differing people with various issues, some known, some not. Since we do not have anything from the other party, we do not always know the complete context of the letter. A one sided conversation is not a good source for doctrine, particularly if that doctrine allegedly opposes or contradicts the foundational Scriptures written by Moses, the Prophets and the Gospels which include the very words of the Messiah.

Sadly, that is what Christianity does with the letters from Paul. Some actually end up following Paul over the Messiah, as if Paul somehow brings newer revelation than the Messiah who lived, died and was resurrected only years earlier. I dare say that if there was some new doctrine or revelation that Elohim planned to transmit to the world, He would have done it through His Son or the disciples of Yahushua.

Instead, Yahushua specifically and unequivocally said: *"[19] Do not think that I came to destroy the Torah or the Prophets. I did not come to destroy but to fulfill. [18] For assuredly, I say to you, till heaven and earth pass away, one jot or one tittle will by no means pass from the law till all is fulfilled."* (Matthew 5:17-18)

He was very clear about the fact that He did not come to change anything. He always obeyed the Commandments and He came to restore and renew the Covenant that had been broken.

The idea that Paul somehow had new revelation to the contrary flies in the very face of all the Scriptures and the history of the Covenant. It is the same argument that Islam uses when it promotes Mohammed as a prophet who brought forth new revelation. They claim to use the same Scriptures as the Jews and the Christians although they have the added texts of the Quran, which alter the previous Scriptures and essentially create a new religion.

To a certain extent, this is what Christianity has done with the writings of Paul and the interpretation of his letters. By elevating the words of Paul over the Words of Elohim, whether they realize it or not, they have made Paul their god.

Of course, part of the problem is that Paul's letters are simply hard to understand. This was specifically provided by Peter who very graciously wrote the following:

> "⁸ But, beloved, do not forget this one thing, that with the Lord one day is as a thousand years, and a thousand years as one day. ⁹ The Lord is not slack concerning His promise, as some count slackness, but is longsuffering toward us, not willing that any should perish but that all should come to repentance. ¹⁰ But the day of the Lord will come as a thief in the night, in which the heavens will pass away with a great noise, and the elements will melt with fervent heat; both the earth and the works that are in it will be burned up. ¹¹ Therefore, since all these things will be dissolved, what manner of persons ought you to be in holy conduct and godliness, ¹² looking for and hastening the coming of the day of God, because of which the heavens will be dissolved, being on fire, and the elements will melt with fervent heat? ¹³ Nevertheless we, according to His promise, look for new heavens and a new earth in which righteousness dwells. ¹⁴ Therefore, beloved, looking forward to these things, be diligent to be found by Him in peace, without spot and

> *blameless; ¹⁵ and consider that the longsuffering of our Lord is salvation - as also our beloved brother Paul, according to the wisdom given to him, has written to you, ¹⁶ <u>as also in all his epistles, speaking in them of these things, in which are some things hard to understand, which untaught and unstable people twist to their own destruction, as they do also the rest of the Scriptures.</u>"* 2 Peter 3:8-16

In this passage, Peter is emphasizing the fact that we cannot be slack, but must continue in holy conduct. Remember that "holy" means "set apart" and this clearly involves righteous living according to the Torah. He is warning of judgment and being found "without spot and blameless." Again, this involves keeping the Commandments. It is the opposite of lawlessness and it is similar to the description of the character of Noah prior to the flood. He was spared because he walked with Elohim.[83]

Peter specifically pointed out that untaught people were twisting Paul's letters along with the Scriptures. They were untaught in the Torah and were obviously using Paul's words as a justification to disobey the Torah. This is exactly what is presently occurring in the Christian religion. The reason it is leading people to destruction is because they are using Paul's letters to justify lawlessness, and we know that lawlessness leads to destruction.

I, myself, do not know Paul, nor do I know who decided to insert Paul's letters into the Bible. What I do know is that the Messiah hand selected twelve disciples who spent years with Him learning from Him and observing Him. He prepared them to take the Good News to the nations.

---

[83] See Genesis 6:9

After the death and resurrection of the Messiah there were eleven remaining and they quickly chose a twelfth – Mathias.[84] Soon after that time they were in Jerusalem celebrating the Appointed Time of Shavuot[85] and the Spirit fell upon those gathered for the Feast. Arguably, Paul would have been there if he were obeying the Commandments,[86] but the Spirit did not fall upon him. Instead, he went about persecuting and killing the followers of Yahushua.

We read about Pentecost in the English translation of Acts chapter 2, a text that initially refers to only a couple of the disciples and then conspicuously places all of the emphasis on Paul, after he claims to have been met by the Messiah in the wilderness on the road to Damascus. There are many who doubt this claim and assert that Paul was "a tare sown among the wheat."

As I said before, I do not know Paul, but whoever compiled the texts that went into the Bible made a specific effort to emphasize Paul and "his gospel" rather than the original disciples of Yahushua. The book of Acts, which ends with Paul, is followed by 14 letters from Paul. Only after all of this emphasis on Paul do we then read 6 short letters, five of them written by the "pillars" of the early Assembly – James, Peter and John.[87]

The emphasis on Paul is the reason why many scholars claim that Paul actually founded the Christian religion. They assert this because the Christian religion has developed most of its doctrine from Paul's letters, rather than the Torah or even the Messiah Yahushua. This is not so evident to a person born and raised in the

---

[84] Acts 1:23-26

[85] Shavuot, also known as Pentecost, is a special Appointed Time that all those in Covenant with Elohim are to observe every year. Shavuot and the other Scriptural Appointed Times are detailed in the Walk in the Light series entitled *Appointed Times*.

[86] This is a safe assumption since Paul described himself "⁵ . . . a Hebrew of the Hebrews, concerning the Torah, a Pharisee; ⁶ concerning zeal, persecuting the church; concerning the righteousness which is in the law, blameless." Philemon 3:5-6

[87] See Galatians 2:9

Christian religion, but to an outsider it is obvious. Indeed, when the Messiah and Paul appear to contradict one another a Christian will almost always defer to the words of Paul over the words of the Messiah.

This is interesting since there is so much controversy and confusion related to Paul. Paul came on the scene rather late in the game. He was not one of the twelve disciples chosen by the Messiah, and Yahushua did not appear to Paul before His ascension. Paul was not among those who were filled with the Spirit on Shavuot. Again, while the disciples of the Messiah were spreading the Good News, Paul was busy persecuting and killing them.

We then read about the "road to Damascus" incident in Acts 9 and Acts 22 where Paul claims to have been blinded by a light. He heard a voice and then devoted his life to promoting what he referred to as "my gospel."[88] Interestingly, these two accounts conflict with one another. In Acts 9:7 he stated that those who travelled with him heard a voice but did not see anyone. In Acts 22:9 he stated that those who travelled with him saw the light but did not hear the voice. So which is it and who were the witnesses?

Now aside from the conflicting story we then need to consider the possibility of a conflicting gospel. Just exactly what Paul meant by "my gospel" is the subject of much debate. Was it the same gospel as taught by the Messiah or was it a different gospel?

Incredibly, Paul places himself in between the Messiah and His followers as he encourages them to "Imitate me, just as I also imitate Christ." (1 Corinthians 11:1)[89] Yahushua repeatedly told His disciples to "Follow Me." If we place our faith and trust in Messiah then we are supposed to follow Him and imitate Him. That is the

---

[88] Romans 2:16, 16:25 and 2 Timothy 2:8
[89] See also 1 Corinthains 4:16 - "*Therefore I urge you, imitate me.*"

traditional relationship between a Rabbi and a disciple. The disciple would live with the Rabbi, listen and observe the Rabbi and become like the Rabbi. So you must ask yourself who you follow and who do you imitate - the Messiah or Paul?

While Christianity has essentially become a Pauline religion, the Messiah did not come to create any new or different religion. He came to restore and renew the ancient Covenant that had been broken. So a person must carefully decide who has the authority.

There are essentially two camps concerning Paul and his writings. Either 1) everything Paul wrote is consistent with the Messiah and his writings are simply misunderstood; or 2) Paul's writings do indeed conflict with the Messiah, but he was commissioned with new revelation and teachings, as if the Messiah passed the baton to Paul to advance a new religion.

Clearly, the second position cannot be correct. In fact, there is little evidence that Paul was commissioned by the Messiah other than Paul's own testimony, recorded by Luke in Acts. It is very interesting to note that Luke wrote Acts. He was not a Yisraelite and he was a friend of Paul. He clearly shifted the emphasis of Acts to Paul with barely a mention of the other disciples. There was certainly a strong bias in favor of Paul, and that is likely attributed to a man rather than the Holy Spirit.

So then the words of Paul are either consistent with the Messiah and His disciples or they are not. We are left with a choice. The problem that Christians must grapple with is how they interpret the texts and what they will chose to obey.

I have a relationship with the Messiah - the One Who renewed the Covenant. I also have a relationship with the Father. As such I obey them - period. I do not have a relationship with Paul. I do not know Him. So if there is any conflict or confusion I will always choose the Messiah - the Word of YHWH over the word of a man, especially if that man tells me to disobey the Commandments.

In fact, we are specifically warned against prophets who would lead us astray. *"¹ If there arises among you a prophet or a dreamer of dreams, and he gives you a sign or a wonder, ² and the sign or the wonder comes to pass, of which he spoke to you, saying, 'Let us go after other gods' - which you have not known = 'and let us serve them,' ³ you shall not listen to the words of that prophet or that dreamer of dreams, for YHWH your Elohim is testing you to know whether you love YHWH your Elohim with all your heart and with all your soul. ⁴ You shall walk after YHWH your Elohim and fear Him, and keep His Commandments and obey His voice; you shall serve Him and hold fast to Him."* (Deuteronomy 13:1-4)

The point is not to get distracted by signs and wonders or led astray from the truth. We are supposed to walk after YHWH and keep His Commandments.

Whether or not Paul is a false prophet does not have to be determined because there is no confusion or debate to be had concerning the truth. The Messiah was very definitive in His words and His purpose. There is no need to add to or take away from any of them.

Interestingly, He was crystal clear regarding the Torah but there are those who simply do not want to obey the Torah. That is why people desperately need Paul and his writings and they also desperately need them to be classified as the "the Word of God." That way they can choose to follow their interpretation of Paul's letters and the lawless path.

Now whether the writings of Paul contradict the Scriptures or whether he has simply been mistranslated or misunderstood is the subject of another book or a volume of books for that matter. The simple point here is that many believe that Paul taught something different than Moses and the Messiah. Therefore you must, in the words of the Patriarch Joshua – *"choose you this day who you will serve."*[90] As for me and my house, we will serve YHWH.

The most significant teaching of Paul that Christians use to justify their disobedience is referred to as grace. A noun that typically refers to favor, mercy, beauty or charm has been expanded to become a doctrine that has completely consumed the Christian religion. Now let us examine the meaning of this very important concept.

---

[90] Joshua 24:15

5

Amazing Grace

Most Christians are familiar with the popular song entitled *Amazing Grace* written by John Newton in the late 1700's. It is a great tune but even the lyrics of this song are reminiscent of Paul as they proclaim "I once was blind but now I see..."

There is no doubt that the writings of Paul have been responsible for the great emphasis placed upon grace. Likely the most common quote repeated by Christians to support their rejection of the Torah comes from Paul. Here is a typical quote: *"For sin shall not have dominion over you, for you are not under law but under grace."* Romans 6:14

This would appear to set grace in direct opposition to the Torah. As a result, it is important to determine what exactly is this concept of grace that would apparently change the entire plan of YHWH, which is to find a people who will obey His Commandments?

The English word grace derives from the Latin gratia, which means gratitude or thanks. This is evident in the Spanish language where "muchas gracias" means "much thanks" or "thanks a lot." When people say grace prior to eating a meal they are supposed to be giving thanks to Elohim for the food.

Yahushua was only recorded as using the word four times, and only in the Book of Luke. In each instance it is used in the context of thanks. Nowhere does Yahushua allude to the notion that the grace of the Elohim would work to abolish His Torah. Sadly this is what is taught and believed throughout much of Christianity.

Here is another quote from Paul that mentions the importance of grace. *"For it is by grace you have been saved, through faith-and this not from yourselves, it is the gift of Elohim"* Ephesians 2:8. So what does this mean? I thought we were saved by the Messiah. How are we now saved by grace?

Simply put, this statement shows that, but for the grace of YHWH, we would not be saved. So grace is not the source of salvation, but rather the response from Elohim that allows for salvation. It is the gift of life that is freely given so that no man would boast that he somehow earned his salvation (Ephesians 2:9).

No man is perfect, save one. Therefore no man can be saved outside of the grace of YHWH. The problem arises when people start treating grace as something new and mutually exclusive from the Torah. They believe that the two are adversarial and that grace has somehow won the struggle and replaced the Torah.

The Greek word which is translated as "grace" in the English language is "charis" (χαριν). The word "charis" (χαριν) is where we derive such words as "charisma" and "charity." It is generally associated with charm or beauty.

The Hebrew word which is often translated in English Bibles as "grace" is "hen" (חן). The word "hen" (חן) means "beauty" or "loveliness." The Hebrew word that most accurately reflects the Christian understanding of "grace" is "hesed" (חשד) which means "goodness" or "kindness," although it is usually translated into English as "mercy." So you can see that the word "grace" has diverse origins and usage, and the original context of the Hebrew has not necessarily been properly represented by using the word "grace." This can lead to some thinking that there was little to no "grace" found in the Hebrew

Scriptures when, in fact, חֶסֶד (hesed) is found 274 times while חֵן (hen) is found only 69 times.

Nelson's Bible Dictionary defines grace as: "Favor or kindness shown without regard to the worth or merit of the one who receives it and in spite of what that same person deserves. Grace is one of the key attributes of [Elohim]. [YHWH Elohim] is 'merciful and gracious, long-suffering, and abounding in goodness and truth' (Exodus 34:6). Therefore, grace is almost always associated with mercy, love, compassion, and patience as the source of help and with deliverance from distress. In the [Tanak], a prime example of grace was the redemption of the Hebrew people from Egypt and their establishment in the Promised Land. This did not happen because of any merit on Israel's part, but in spite of their unrighteousness (Deuteronomy 9:5-6). Although the grace of [Elohim] is always free and undeserved, it must not be taken for granted. Grace is only enjoyed within the Covenant - the gift is given by [Elohim], and the gift is received by man through repentance and faith (Amos 5:15). Grace is to be humbly sought through the prayer of faith (Malachi 1:9). The grace of [Elohim] was supremely revealed and given in the person and work of [Yahushua Messiah]. [Yahushua] was not only the beneficiary of [Elohim's] grace (Luke 2:40), but He was also its very embodiment (John 1:14), bringing it to mankind for salvation (Titus

2:11). By His death and resurrection, [Yahushua] restored the broken fellowship between Elohim and His people, both Jew and Gentile.[91]

This is a reasonably thorough and accurate definition, although not all Christian Bible Commentaries are so good. Read the following definition of grace from another commentary:

> Grace - salvation by grace in the New Testament is opposed to an Old Testament doctrine of salvation by works (Romans 4:4; 11:6), or, what is the same thing, by law.[92]

Sadly, this comment is absolutely false – Yisrael was never saved by their obedience to the Torah. While it was considered righteousness for them to observe the Torah they were never justified by their works.[93] In fact, few people even realize that the Temple Sacrificial system only provided atonement for unintentional sin. There is no specified sacrifice for intentional sin outside of the mercy of YHWH.

Interestingly, when we are provided this information in the Scriptures we are told that the Torah is the same for a native born or a stranger who dwells in the assembly. *"*[14] *And if a stranger dwells with you, or whoever is among you throughout your generations, and would present an offering made by fire, a sweet aroma to YHWH, just as you do, so shall he do.* [15] *One ordinance shall be for you*

---

[91] Nelson's Illustrated Bible Dictionary, Copyright (c) 1986, Thomas Nelson Publishers. Note - corrected names and spellings added for consistency and accuracy.
[92] International Standard Bible Encyclopaedia, Electronic Database Copyright (c) 1996 by Biblesoft.
[93] Deuteronomy 6:25. The shedding of the blood of animals provided for atonement, which means: "covering." It did not provide a washing away of sins.

of the assembly and for the stranger who dwells with you, an ordinance forever throughout your generations; as you are, so shall the stranger be before YHWH. ¹⁶ One Torah and one custom shall be for you and for the stranger who dwells with you" (Numbers 15:14-16)

A little further in the same portion of Scripture we are told: "*You shall have one Torah for him who sins unintentionally, for him who is native-born among the children of Yisrael and for the stranger who dwells among them.*" (Numbers 15:29)

Thus it was always understood that the Torah was for all people who desired to dwell with YHWH and obedience to the Torah did not bring about salvation. There remained the unresolved issue of intentional sin which leads to death. It was also understood that we needed the unmerited favor - hesed - of the Almighty to live. This is what Christianity commonly refers to as grace.

It is only through the "hesed" of the Almighty that we are offered the free gift of life everlasting. This unmerited favor resulted from something that YHWH did – there was nothing we could do to earn it.

This fact was specifically revealed during the original blood Covenant made between YHWH and Abram. During that Covenant process Abram was placed in a deep sleep and only YHWH passed through the pieces and the blood. This meant that only YHWH was responsible for the punishment associated with the breaking of the Covenant. Later, when Abraham was told to offer up his son, YHWH stopped him and revealed that He would provide the sacrifice.[94] In each instance, we see the "hesed" or grace of YHWH revealed through the Covenant.

There is nothing that Torah observance can do to

---

[94] The covenant process and the patterns provided through the Scriptural Covenants are detailed in the Walk in the Light series book entitled *Covenants*.

earn that gift. What is required is the same faith that Abraham demonstrated. We need to believe the promises of YHWH - the promises that were provided through His Covenant - and we need to demonstrate our belief through our actions. *"For as the body without the spirit is dead, so faith without works is dead also"* (James 2:26)

The question that remains is: What do we do once we receive the gift and enter into the Renewed Covenant provided through the blood of the Messiah? That, of course, is the issue faced by every Christian.

Our response, as we have already seen, should then be obedience to Torah. You see, grace and Torah operate together in perfect harmony. The Torah shows us that we need favor and once we receive the gift freely given we should naturally walk in the ways of the Torah as an expression of our love and appreciation.

Sadly the paradigm that the Torah and Grace are opposed to one another has been perpetuated by countless books, sermons and commentaries as well as erroneous Scriptural translations.

Grace is not some new concept introduced in the New Testament - it is evident from the beginning of creation. The fact that we were created and given the breath of life is the ultimate act of beauty and kindness provided by the Creator. He then gave man dominion over creation - again grace. In fact, once you shift your inherited paradigm you will find grace throughout the Scriptures.

It is evident from the lives of men such as Noah and Abraham. They believed in the promises of YHWH. They put their faith and trust in YHWH and their faith was counted toward righteousness. Their obedience then led to their being blessed.

The Scriptures record that: *"Noah found grace in the eyes of YHWH."* (Genesis 6:8) In other words, YHWH looked favorably upon Noah because he was an obedient and righteous man. The reason why he found favor was because of how he lived. The Scriptures record: "**Noah was a just man, perfect in his generations. Noah walked with Elohim.**" (Genesis 6:9) This clearly reveals that Noah obeyed the Commandments. That is exactly what it means to "walk with Elohim."

Therefore, his obedience led to the deliverance and salvation of mankind. He believed YHWH <u>and</u> he acted upon the instructions, which saved him and his family from judgment. Could it be any clearer?

Abraham's faith was counted toward righteousness and he is renowned for his life of obedience.[95] The Scriptures also record that Yisrael's observance of YHWH's commands and their fear of YHWH was accounted as righteousness to them; both of which signal faith and belief.

"*[24] And YHWH commanded us to observe all these statutes, to fear YHWH our Elohim, for our good always, that He might preserve us alive, as it is this day.[25] Then it will be righteousness for us, if we are careful to observe all these commandments before YHWH our Elohim, as He has commanded us.*" (Deuteronomy 6:24-25)

Moses viewed grace as a sort of prerequisite for knowing the Ways of YHWH, which allowed him to know the Almighty. "*[13] <u>Now therefore, I pray, if I have found grace in Your sight, show me now Your way, that I may know You and that I may find grace in Your sight.</u> And consider that this nation is Your people. [14] And He said, 'My Presence will go with you, and I will give you rest.'*" (Exodus 33:12-14)

This should be our yearning as well. Mosheh asked for grace and he received the Presence of YHWH and His rest. We read also: "*[8] So Mosheh made haste and bowed his head toward the earth, and worshiped. [9] Then he said, 'If now I have found grace in Your sight, O Adonai, let*

---

[95] Genesis 15:6

my Adonai, I pray, go among us, even though we are a stiff-necked people; and <u>pardon our iniquity and our sin, and take us as Your inheritance</u>.'" (Exodus 34:8-9)

Grace in these passages clearly means: "favor." Now with that understanding let us again consider the previously mentioned quote from Paul and instead of the English word grace, let us use the word favor.

"For sin shall not have dominion over you, for you are not under law but under <u>favor</u>." (Romans 6:14) The verse should now be much clearer. In fact, when we review the context of the passage we see that it is all about not sinning.

"¹² Therefore do not let sin reign in your mortal body, that you should obey it in its lusts. ¹³ And do not present your members as instruments of unrighteousness to sin, but present yourselves to Elohim as being alive from the dead, and your members as instruments of righteousness to Elohim. ¹⁴ For sin shall not have dominion over you, for you are not under law but under grace." (Romans 6:12-14)

We know that sin is defined as a violation of the Torah. So the statement was all about the grace, or rather favor of YHWH, helping is to obey the Torah. In other words, we are not under the punishment that the Torah prescribes for sin "thanks" to the shed blood of the Messiah. We now receive favor because of what He did for us.

Paul had to mean that because the very next verse clarifies the intent by proclaiming: *"What then? Shall we sin because we are not under law but under grace? Certainly not!"* (Romans 6:15)

So Paul is stating that we should definitely not sin, just because we receive favor. The only way not to sin is to walk according to the instruction of the Torah. Therefore, it does not appear that Paul actually intended to assert that grace trumped or replaced the Torah. Sadly, grace has been treated as something diametrically opposed to the Torah, which is a grievous mistake.

Without the Torah as a foundation, grace has become a license to sin for many. The Torah provided the framework within which mankind was intended to live from the very beginning in the Garden of Eden. In fact, the word garden in Hebrew is "gan" (גן) which specifically refers to a place that is fenced in or hedged about. Thus when mankind lived in the garden he was living within the boundaries of the Torah.

Since the transgression in the garden and the expulsion of Adam and Hawah, we all need favor to restore us into right relationship with our Creator thus - grace is the starting point of our journey of restoration. When we receive favor and forgiveness we can then obey the Torah and when we stumble, we are not under the punishment prescribed by the Torah but we have atonement by the blood of the Lamb. This is the grace that Paul was talking about.

It reopens the entranceway to the garden that was once closed to mankind. It is because of grace that we can become cleansed from our sins and endeavor upon a life of obedience to the Torah, not the other way around. The Torah shows us how to walk and be blessed through the favor of Elohim, but many miss those blessings because they are walking outside of the protective hedge of the garden - outside of the Torah - outside of the Covenant.

So how did the Christian stray so far from this fundamental precept? The answer to that question can be discerned when we look back to the origins of Christianity.

6

Christianity

Here's a news flash - Jesus was not a Christian. He was a Torah observant Yisraelite from the Tribe of Judah. He was a Jew,[96] but only in the sense that He was from the Tribe of Judah. He did not subscribe to the religion of Judaism.[97] That is because the religion that we now know as Judiasm did not exist at the time. Judaism is a religion that was developed by the Pharisees after the Temple was destroyed by the Romans in 70 CE. It became a religion in an effort to replace the Temple service and perpetuate the faith of Yisrael.

While the Torah is still supposed to be at the heart of Judaism, it is a religion developed and controlled by the Pharisaic traditions. Remember that the Pharisees were only one of many sects of Yisraelites. They did not represent all Yisraelites, nor did they have a monopoly on the faith. The priests were supposed to be the teachers of Yisrael.

So while Yahushua was Jewish in the sense that He came from the tribe of Judah, He was not a practicing Jew as we see Judaism today. He was simply a Yisraelite

---

[96] As was already mentioned in Footnote 40, the term "Jew" derives from the name Judah. It historically referred to those who descend from the Tribe of Judah or at some point joined with the Tribe of Judah. It also referenced a person who came from the region known as Judea. Currently, it applies to those who ascribe to the religion of Judaism or identify with the culture and progeny of the ancient Kingdom of Judah.

[97] The religion of Judaism did not officially begin until after the destruction of the temple in 70 CE. Prior to that time the faith of Yisrael revolved around the Temple and the Priesthood. After the destruction of the Temple, the Pharisees took over the faith and developed Rabbinic Judaism that was controlled by Rabbinic rules, regulations and traditions.

– the Messiah of Yisrael. He renewed the Covenant with Yisrael and those who follow Him and join into His Renewed Covenant are all Yisraelites – not Christians.

The religion of Christianity did not form until over three hundred years after the death of Yahushua. It was established by the Roman Empire. Originally, all of the followers of the Messiah were Yisraelites. It only makes sense that those in Covenent with YHWH and anticipating a Messiah would be the first to receive Him. Only later would the Gentiles be drawn into the Assembly. This was the pattern that was always supposed to occur.

The word "Gentiles" is a very misunderstood term. It essentially means: "nations." It separates the Assembly of Yisrael from all others. There are those who follow YHWH – Yisrael, and there are all others – Gentiles. Another equivalent term is "heathens." The nations are the ones who do not walk according to the instructions and Commandments of YHWH. Currently, the word "pagan" is treated as an equivalent to the word "heathen."

So you don't want to be a Gentile, and if you are born a Gentile, outside of the Covenant, you want to get into the Covenant. That is what Yahushua came to do. He renewed the Covenant and made a way for the lost sheep of the House of Yisrael to be restored to the Covenant. Through that process the Nations would be drawn into the Covenant.

Previously, the religious leaders of Yisrael had literally and figuratively built a wall of separation between Yisrael and the Nations. Instead of drawing the Nations to the Creator and bringing them into the fold, the religious ones built walls and put up obstacles for the Gentiles.

Judaism continues this practice of the Pharisees. They have developed a "us versus them" mentality, and if you want to obey the Torah they claim that you have to become a Jew and follow the rules and regulations of Judaism. It is essentially an attempted Pharisaic takeover of the identity and faith of Yisrael.

Of course this is the main reason why Yahushua strongly opposed the Pharisees and that is why they wanted to kill Him. He challenged their authority and they hated Him for that. They developed their own conversion process for Gentiles which was not the method prescribed by YHWH.

Foreigners and strangers were always welcome to join into the Covenant with Yisrael. All they had to do was obey and become circumcised. They had to receive the mark, or rather "sign" of the Covenant on their bodies and live out the sign of the Covenant - the Sabbath and the Torah. They did not convert to Judaism, rather they joined with Yisrael.

The Pharisees were building a religion and they developed their own conversion process. They were not so much concerned about drawing the Nations to YHWH as they were to getting other Yisraelites to live like them. They were a type of "holiness" movement primarily concerned with behavior, and the Pharisees sought to instill their form of life on other Jews. Much of it focused on outward appearance.

One of their primary forms of "evangelism" was through table fellowship. "The Pharisees' gathering together to eat properly tithed food in a state of ritual purity, and the procedures for acquiring food and maintaining households or other spaces fit for such gatherings, were strategies to influence non-Pharisees to conform to a Pharisaic way of life."[98]

The Pharisaic conversion process was focused on

---

[98] *Were the Pharisees a Conversionist Sect? Table Fellowship as a Strategy of Conversion* © Jonathan D. Brumberg-Kraus, Wheaton College 2002 referencing Gerd Theissen, *The Sociology of Early Palestinian Christianity* (Philadelphia: Fortress, 1978), pp. 77-99.

getting people to conform to their behavioral norms, which included rules and regulations that went beyond the Torah. Again, they added to the Torah. With that understanding it is interesting to see the various confrontations between the Messiah and the Pharisees at a table or involving tithing or food. He was critiquing and tampering with their primary conversion tool and they did not like that.

This was the main point of contention between the Pharisees and Yahushua. He refused to follow their rules, laws and traditions. He challenged their authority and rebuked them for adding to the Torah. They hated Him because He refused to follow the Torah within their prescribed religious paradigm.[99]

Sadly, the strife did not end after the death and resurrection of Yahushua. You might think that would have settled the issue once and for all, but religious men will stubbornly hold on to their religious ways if they do not have hearts to obey. Religions are in many ways a test of the heart. Will we follow YHWH or will we follow the traditions and mandates of man-made religious systems? While many Yisraelites chose to follow the Messiah, others remained grounded in their traditions.

What eventually resulted was that the followers of Yahsuhua became a separate sect within the Yisraelite community. Those under the authority of the Messiah became known as the Notzrim, also known as the Nazareans.

Initially, these Nazareans were all native

---

[99] Not much has changed over the centuries. I myself have experienced some of that same hatred as some from Judaism have lashed out because I teach others the Commandments in the same way that Yahushua taught them. I oppose the notion that you must convert to Judaism in order to obey the Commandments. Of course, this is contrary to popular Jewish thought that the Torah is only for the Jews and non-Jews cannot obey the Torah. You see if you obey the Torah outside of Judaism then you are not under Rabbinic authority and authority, after all, is at the heart of the matter.

Yisraelites and they would still assemble at the Temple and in the Synagogues, but that did not last for long. The followers of Yahushua ended up following His mandate to go into all of the world[100] and they began bringing Gentiles into the Assembly.

Again, they were not converting Gentiles to Judaism or Christianity – neither of these religions officially existed at that time. Instead, they were fishing for "the lost sheep of the house of Yisrael"[101] and drawing them back into the Assembly of Yisrael. This became a main point of contention between the Nazarean sect and the Pharisaic sect. The Pharisees had a complex conversion ritual which the Nazareans specifically rejected.[102]

Over the centuries, the divisions between the sects persisted and grew to the point where today we see two separate and distinct religions which both claim to worship the same Elohim. What we now call Judaism traces back directly to the Pharisee sect.

After the Temple was destroyed in 70 C.E., by the Roman forces under the command of Titus, the Pharisees became the predominant sect of Yisraelites. The followers of Yahushua had already heeded the words of Yahushua and fled the Land of Judea before the invading army of the Romans had captured and destroyed Jerusalem.[103]

---

[100] Matthew 28:19, Mark 16:15

[101] Yahushua was fulfilling the prophecy in Jeremiah 16:16 that stated: "*Behold, I will send for many fishermen, says YHWH, and they shall fish them . . .*" This is why Yahushua specifically selected several fishermen for His disciples. He told them that He would make them "fishers of men" in order to fulfill this prophecy (see Matthew 4:19 and Mark 1:17). This was ultimately revealed to the disciples after the resurrection when He appeared to them at the Sea of Galilee while they were fishing. He directed them to cast their nets on the right side of their boat and they drew in 153 large fish (John 21:6-11). In the Hebrew language every letter has an equivalent numerical value and 153 equals "the Sons of Elohim." This was a direct reference to the Hosea 1:10 prophecy concerning the House of Yisrael.

[102] See Acts 15

[103] "[20] *But when you see Jerusalem surrounded by armies, then know that its desolation is near.* [21] *Then let those who are in Judea flee to the mountains, let those who are in the midst of her*

The Pharisees who did not follow the Messiah remained and were nearly exterminated. Those who survived brokered an agreement with the Romans and were permitted to establish a new religious "headquarters" at Yavneh. Jerusalem was made into a desolation and with no Temple the Sadducees practically disappeared.

The Zealots, who actively fought against the Romans, were scattered and decimated leaving the Pharisees as the only significant identifiable sect of Yisraelites remaining in the Land. This was the beginning of Rabbinic Judaism. With all of the competing Yisraelite sects gone, the Rabbis assumed full authority over interpreting the Scriptures and over the people.

With this understanding it should now be easier to understand that while modern Judaism has ancient roots, contrary to popular belief, it is not what Mosheh taught in the Torah and certainly not what Yahushua practiced and taught.

Much of Judaism is based upon Talmudic Law[104] rather than strictly YHWH's Torah. This is an error and it is the same reason why Yahushua rebuked the Pharisees by asking: *"Why do you also transgress the Commandment of Elohim because of your tradition?"* (Matthew 15:3)

The Pharisees had been teaching their traditions

---

depart, and let not those who are in the country enter her. [22] *For these are the days of vengeance, that all things which are written may be fulfilled."* Luke 21:20-22

[104] The Talmud is a Hebrew word that means: "instruction, learning" and it comes from a root *that* means "teach, study." It is a central text of Rabbinic Judaism. The term "Talmud" normally refers to the collection of writings named specifically the Babylonian Talmud *(Talmud Bavli)*, although there is also an earlier collection known as the Jerusalem Talmud, or Palestinian Talmud *(Talmud Yerushalmi)*. The entire Talmud consists of 63 tractates, and in standard print is over 6,200 pages long. It is written in Tannaitic Hebrew and Aramaic, and contains the teachings and opinions of thousands of rabbis (dating from before the Christian Era through the fifth century CE) on a variety of subjects, including Halakha (law), Jewish ethics, philosophy, customs, history, lore and many other topics. The Talmud is the basis for all codes of Jewish law, and is widely quoted in rabbinic literature. Quoted from Wikipedia

as if they carried the same or more weight than the Commandments. At the same time, they were neglecting the Commands of Elohim. This became increasingly more prevalent once they moved to Yavneh.

Judaism now claims to represent the same faith as ancient Yisrael, but this is not the case. It is simply a surviving sect of many different competing sects of Yisrael. The religion of Judaism, as we see it today, does not equate to the Assembly of Yisrael - nor does the religion of Christianity for that matter. You do not have to convert to Judaism or Christianity to become part of Yisrael because currently, neither of these religions accurately represents the Assembly of Yisrael.

The religion of Christianity was created hundreds of years after the destruction of Jerusalem. While it can also be traced to a sect of Yisrael consisting of the followers of Yahushua, it ended up incorporating many of the pagan elements from the environment in which it developed - the Roman Empire.

The Christian religion is not the same faith lived and taught by Yahushua and His disciples. In fact, there was no such religion as Christianity when Yahushua walked the earth, nor did He create a new religion after His death and resurrection. Likewise, the Christian religion did not exist during the lives of the original disciples nor did they create a new religion or convert people to Christianity. The early disciples were all Yisraelites and they never converted to any new religion - they always maintained their original faith based upon the Torah.

Most students of the Christian religion are taught that Roman Emperor Constantine "converted" to Christianity and from that point on Christianity became the official state religion of the Roman Empire. What most are not taught is that Constantine was a Mithra worshipper until the day he died. He had his wife and child murdered after his so-called conversion and he had a mother who used sorcery and divination to locate all of the Christian Holy Places. Constantine did not convert to Christianity – he created the religion as we now know it!

A closer analysis of history reveals that it was that period of time when the original faith was repackaged into a new religion. This new religion was littered with heresy from the very beginning. It turns out that the "conversion" of Constantine was a political tactic to save his declining Empire and it actually worked for a time.

Read what M. Turretin, wrote in describing the state of Christianity in the 4th century, saying, "that it was not so much the [Roman] Empire that was brought over to the Faith, as the Faith was brought over to the Empire; not the Pagans who were converted to Christianity, but Christianity that was converted to Paganism."

Emperor Constantine was responsible for salvaging the faltering Roman Empire through reconstruction, including making Christianity the official state religion of the Roman Empire - most notably through The Council of Nicaea in 325 C.E. The official state religion created by Constantine is what we now know as the Roman Catholic Church.

Despite his claims of conversion, it is doubtful that his apparent change of faith was anything but a political maneuver or an act of syncretism, which the Catholic Church has been renowned for throughout its existence (i.e. the blending of pagan faiths with the Christian or Catholic doctrine). We know this because he actually had a coin minted which depicts himself on one side and Mithra on the other side with the statement: SOLI INVICTO COMITI - Committed to the Invincible Sun.

After this not so illustrious beginning, centuries later we see that the Christian religion, having now splintered into countless denominations, has remained a repository for paganism and various cultic beliefs. At its very core is a belief in Jesus the Christ which has become quite different than the original faith which followed Yahushua the Messiah of Yisrael. This is not just a difference in words or languages – there are critical and fundamental differences between the faith lived and taught by the original disciples and modern Christians.

It is not the same assembly that received the outpouring of the Spirit at the Appointed Time of Shavuot in Jerusalem, popularly known as Pentecost, after the resurrection of the Messiah. While Christianity often claims to have picked up where Yisrael left off, this is a false doctrine called Replacement Theology. Yisrael is still the community of faith and the Christian "church" has not replaced Yisrael.

Thus we see two religions, Christianity and Judaism, both laying claim to the same Elohim, stumbling through the centuries to this point in history where they find their destinies converging like the two sticks becoming one as prophesied in Ezekiel 37:19. Although these two religions have shared common roots, and even common Scriptures, they have also been divided by a seeming unsurpassable chasm, and neither actually obeys the Commandments of Elohim.

The people of Elohim were never meant to remain divided into different nations, religions or denominations. The path to Elohim was always through a Covenant relationship centered upon the Commandments. It did not matter whether you were a native-born Yisraelite or a stranger drawn to YHWH from the Nations.

This is evident from the command given to Yisrael that "*one Torah shall be for the native-born and for* *the stranger who dwells among you." (Exodus 12:49) "*^{14}* And if a stranger dwells with you, or whoever is among you throughout your generations, and would present an offering made by fire, a sweet aroma to YHWH, just as you do, so shall he do.*^{15}* one ordinance shall be for you of the assembly and for the stranger who dwells with you, an ordinance forever throughout your generations; as you are, so shall the stranger be before YHWH.*^{16}* <u>one Torah and one custom shall be for you and for the stranger who dwells with you</u>." (Numbers 15:14-16)

In other words, anyone who wanted to worship the Elohim of Yisrael and dwell in the Kingdom was subject to the same Torah as a native-born Yisraelite. There was no distinction made in the Torah concerning how people worshipped Elohim, they all had to do it in the same way - His way.

One of the great problems is the use of semantics. Just as the terms Jew and Gentile have been used to create division between Judaism and Christianity, so we see the notion of "The Church" exascerbating the problem. Christianity promotes the idea that "The Church" is now a set apart assembly that is separate and distinct from the Assembly of YHWH, which He calls Yisrael.

As long as people continue to use the terms Church and Yisrael as mutually exclusive groups, you are always going to have division and people will run into confusion when attempting to interpret the Scriptures, just as occurs by the misuse of the terms Jew and Gentile. It is critical to understand that Yisrael does not belong to the religion of Judaism, nor has it been replaced by the Christian Church.

The word "church" is not found anywhere in the Hebrew or Greek manuscripts of the Scriptures. It is a man-made word that has been inserted into the English translations of the New Testament texts whenever they refer to the set apart assembly of YHWH described in Greek as the "ekklesia" (εκκλεσια) and in Hebrew as the "qahal" (קהל). As a result of this translation issue, many Believers see this new entity, "the church" in the New Testament texts which does not appear in the Old Testament and they understandably assume that it must be something newly established by the Messiah.

Looking at the word "church," we see that Christianity uses it in a variety of contexts. Christians often refer to the Church as a whole of both living and non-living believers. The Church is often used in conjunction with "the Body of Christ" or "the Bride of Christ." It can mean an individual body of believers in a country, state or other geographical entity. It is also often used to refer to a building where Christians assemble.

So where does this word church come from? It does not appear once in the Old Testament and yet when you look in the New Testament it is found throughout the text. The sudden appearance of this new concept would lead the average reader to think that the concept of the Church must be something new, after all it is in the New Testament so that presumption seems to make sense.

Probably the most frequently quoted passage concerning the establishment of the Church is when Yahushua told Peter: "*Upon this rock I will build My church.*" (Matthew 16:18) He was referring, of course, to the revelation that Peter spoke regarding the fact that Yahushua is the Messiah. While we read the word "church" in English He actually declared that upon that truth He would build "*My House of Prayer*" (בית תפלתי).[105]

Yahushua never said the word "church" because it did not exist when He spoke those memorable words to Peter. You will only read the word "church" in an English translation, not a Hebrew or Greek manuscript

---

[105] See George Howard's translation of the Hebrew Gospel of Matthew

of Matthew. The only other reference in the Gospels which attributes the word church to Yahushua is also found in Matthew as follows: *"And if he shall neglect to hear them, tell it unto the church: but if he neglect to hear the church, let him be unto thee as an heathen man and a publican."* (Matthew 18:17 KJV) In this passage the Hebrew refers to "qahal" (קהל) instead of "church."

Again, the word "qahal" (קהל) is the same word used throughout the Scriptures to describe Yisrael as a set apart assembly or congregation. Yahushua was advising people to take their dispute to the "assembly" - not the Christian Church or local church building on the corner - neither of which existed when He made that statement.

This point becomes even clearer when we look at the Septuagint, which is the Greek translation of the Old Testament. In the Septuagint we see that the word "ekklesia" (εκκλεσια) was used in place of the Hebrew word "qahal" (קהל). So the Greek word "ekklesia" was considered to mean the same thing as the Hebrew "qahal" and they almost always were used to refer to the set apart Assembly of Yisrael.

The Greek word "ekklesia" (εκκλεσια) derives from a compound of "ek" (εκ); a primary preposition denoting origin, from, out of place, time, or cause and a derivative of "kaleo" (καλεο); to "call." Therefore, the word "ekklesia" (εκκλεσια) is a "calling out" or rather "a called out assembly." So what is traditionally translated as "church" should actually be translated "called out assembly" or "called out congregation."

According to Fausset's Bible Dictionary the word "church" comes from the Greek "kuriakee" (κυριακεε) - 'House of the lord' - a word which passed to the Gothic tongue. The Goths being the first of the northern hordes converted to Christianity, adopted the word from the Greek Christians of Constantinople, and so it came to us

- 84 -

Anglo-Saxons.[106] In fact, the word derives from "circus" or "kirk," which mean "circle," because the oldest temples, as the Druid ones, were circular in form. So then the word "church" is actually reminiscent of pagan temples.

The word "ekklesia" in the New Testament texts would never mean a building or house of assembly, because "church" buildings were built long after the Scriptures were written. The early believers met in houses, at the Temple in Jerusalem or at a synagogue. The word "synagogue" is really just a Greek word for a place of gathering and prayer.

It is important to remember that there is only one Temple and the bottom line is that there is no such thing as a church that is separate from Yisrael. There is only one Kingdom and the Kingdom Assembly is still called Yisrael.[107]

So Christianity has become a separate and distinct religion that has strayed far from the Messiah that they claim to follow. His identity and teachings have been confused, distorted and hidden. His name has been changed and the Christian religion has transformed him into a lawless pagan christ.

Again, those who refuse to use the proper Hebrew Name of the Messiah and insist upon calling Him by an English name are not being intellectually honest. The reason is that the English equivalent to Yahushua is Joshua, not Jesus. Now I am not encouraging people to call the Messiah Joshua, because I do not believe that

---

[106] See Trench, Study of Words

[107] This is where it gets confusing because we currently have a nation called Israel in the Middle East, formed under seemingly incredible circumstances. Authorized by the United Nations in 1947 and later declaring its independence in 1948, the modern State of Israel was specifically intended to be a Jewish State premised upon the nationalistic and political movement of Zionism. While it may contain some who belong to the assembly of Yisrael, the nation itself is not the set apart Covenant Assembly of Yisrael.

names should change from one language to another. They may be transliterated, but they should always sound the same.

Remember that English is a relatively fledgling language, historically speaking. The letter "J" is an advent of the English language and did not exist in any of the ancient languages such as Hebrew, Aramaic, Greek or Latin. Therefore, it is philologically impossible for the name of the Hebrew Messiah from the Tribe of Judah, more accurately pronounced Yahudah, to be named Jesus.

The simple fact is that the Messiah was never called Jesus when He walked the Earth. His Name was not, is not, nor ever will be Jesus. It was and remains Yahushua and if you refuse to recognize this irrefutable historical fact then you are ironically committing the same sin as the Pharisees. You have chosen a tradition over truth and your choice is a direct affront to the Messiah.

It is not just the letter "J" that is the problem. There is also no etymological connection between the English name Jesus and the Hebrew name Yahushua. In fact, the name Jesus derives from the Greek Iesus, which is directly related to a mythological child of Zeus.[108] What we see in the Christian representation of the Messiah is more blending of pagan sun worship and that

---

[108] Iesus was actually a healing deity, so it is not difficult to understand how the Messiah could get tagged with this name. Especially when one recognizes that the original faith in the Messiah grew in ranks by incorporating converted pagans. These pagans often came loaded with certain "baggage" and ended up blending their pagan practices and ideas with their newly found faith. This is how the Gnostics became so prevalent early on. The Greek New Testament manuscripts actually replace the name of Elijah with Helios, a pagan sun god. This is because they both had stories relating to riding a chariot into the heavens. As a result, the pagans replaced an unfamiliar Hebrew name with a familiar pagan name. This is not proper, but it was done. The Roman Catholic Church has a well established history of adopting and transforming the customs of their pagan converts, and blending them into their traditions. This practice is known as "syncretism." So things have been altered and changed to suit the needs of converts. Regrettably, this is an undeniable fact. The subject is discussed further in the Walk in the Light series books entitled *Restoration* and *Names*.

is a difficult thing for most Jews to get past. To them, Christianity is very much a pagan religion. Sadly, the Name of the Messiah is not the only Babylonian influence that exists in the Christian religion.

As mentioned previously, the Christian religion celebrates the birth of the Messiah on Christmas, which is a Babylonian derived tradition associated with the winter solstice. Most all sun worshippers around the world and through the ages believed that the sun god was born, or reborn, on December 25th, the winter solstice. The winter solstice now falls on December 21st, but at the time that the Babylonian traditions originated it was December 25th. Yahushua, the Messiah of Yisrael, was actually born on an Appointed Time of YHWH.[109]

The Christian religion also celebrates the resurrection of the Messiah on Easter. Easter is the name of a Babylonian derived sun goddess and it is an annual pagan fertility celebration.[110] This is why rabbits and eggs remain part of the Easter traditions. They are fertility symbols.

Of course, the inclusion of Babylonian sun worship within the religion of Christianity should be no surprise to anyone who recognizes that Christianity traces directly to the Roman Empire - not the Messiah.

The Christian religion instituted by the Roman Empire was very different from the Covenant faith of Yisrael lived and taught by the Messiah. In fact, it was a counterfeit religion that quickly separated from the Covenant faith of YHWH found in the Torah.

It is actually opposed to the Commandments of

---

[109] The Messiah was born on the Appointed Time known as Yom Teruah, the Day of Blasting, sometimes called Rosh HaShanah which means: "the head of the year." This memorializes Day 1 of Creation when the light was caused to shine in the darkness. The birth of Yahushua is discussed in detail in the Walk in the Light series book entitled *The Messiah*.

[110] The incorporation of pagan celebrations into the religion of Christianity is discussed in the Walk in the Light series books entitled *Restoration* and *Pagan Holidays*.

YHWH set forth in the Torah. That is why most Christians are directed away from the Torah. They call it the "Old Testament" and most do not feel that they should obey the righteous Commandments of YHWH found in the Torah. This is a fundamental tenet of Christianity espoused through the notion of "grace."[III]

The Christian religion has also seriously misrepresented the teachings of Yahushua. He came preaching repentance, which involved a return to YHWH and His Commandments.[112] Recall one of His first recorded teachings when He proclaimed:

> "[17] Do not think that I came to destroy the Torah or the Prophets. I did not come to destroy but to fulfill. [18] For assuredly, I say to you, till heaven and earth pass away, one jot or one tittle will by no means pass from the Torah till all is fulfilled. [19] Whoever therefore breaks one of the least of these Commandments, and teaches men so, shall be called least in the Kingdom of Heaven; but whoever does and teaches them, he shall be called great in the Kingdom of Heaven. [20] For I say to you, that unless your righteousness exceeds the righteousness of the scribes and Pharisees, you will by no means enter the Kingdom of Heaven." Matthew 5:17-20

[III] Most Christians are taught, and generally believe, that the Messiah did away with the Torah through "grace." This is contrary to the express statement of Messiah when He stated: "[17] Do not think that I came to destroy the Torah or the Prophets. I did not come to destroy but to fulfill. [18] For assuredly, I say to you, till heaven and earth pass away, one jot or one tittle will by no means pass from the law till all is fulfilled." Matthew 5:17-18. His fulfillment of the Torah and the Prophets has nothing to do with destroying or doing away with them. The Torah and the Prophets exist and are relevant until heaven and earth pass away, whenever that is. We can state for certain that that time has not yet arrived. This subject is discussed in detail in the Walk in the Light series book entitled *The Law and Grace*.

[112] Matthew 4:17

Yahushua specifically stated that He did not come to destroy the Torah, but that is exactly what many teach that He did. To the contrary, He came to fulfill the Torah by living it as YHWH intended. As the Word of Elohim, He provided the example. You see the Pharisees had disobeyed the express commandment not to add to or take away from the Torah.[113]

They had added to and taken away from the Torah by their traditions, which were treated as if they were "Law." They were promoting and teaching their own traditions as being equal or above the Commandments of YHWH. This was the issue at the heart of much of the controversy that Yahushua had with them.[114] That is why He proclaimed that your righteousness must exceed that of the Pharisees. They were deriving their righteousness from their traditions. As a result, they are not getting into the Kingdom. True righteousness is found in the Torah just as Yahushua taught and lived.

While many of the Jews believed in Yahushua and followed Him, the Pharisees remained a separate sect of Yisrael that generally opposed the authority of Yahushua. After the destruction of the Temple in 70 CE, the Pharisees became the predominate sect of Yisraelites apart from the followers of Yahushua, who were sometimes called Natzrenes.

This is where history and division take over. Each sect ultimately formed a new religion, separate and apart from the original faith of Yahushua and the Covenant path that YHWH established for Yisrael. The Pharisees established the religion of Judaism. The Natzrenes ended

---

[113] Deuteronomy 4:2, 12:32
[114] A good example of the controversy between Yahushua and the Pharisees can be seen in Mark 7. The Pharisees were criticizing Yahushua and His disciples for not following the tradition concerning the washing of hands. Yahushua rebuked them for rejecting the commandments and holding to their traditions. They had essentially elevated their traditions over the simple commandments of YHWH.

up becoming overrun with Gentiles who diluted the faith until the Roman Empire developed the religion of Christianity. Christianity originated as a blending of the Natzrene faith and sun worship.

Christianity, as we see it today, does not represent the walk that Yahushua taught. It claims a separate and distinct identity from Yisrael, which has no basis in the Scriptures. The Covenant flowed from Abram to Yisrael. Yisrael always represented the Covenant people of YHWH. Just because they broke the Covenant does not mean that YHWH is finished with them. In fact, it was specifically revealed that YHWH, through His Son, would bear the punishment for their breaking the Covenant.[115]

Yisrael, after all, was the Bride of YHWH. While she was divided and punished, the prophecies promised a regathering and reuniting through the Messiah. Here is one of many prophecies attesting to that fact.

> "*21 Then say to them, Thus says the Master YHWH: 'Surely I will take the children of Yisrael from among the nations, wherever they have gone, and will gather them from every side and bring them into their own land; 22 and I will make them one nation in the land, on the mountains of Yisrael; and one king shall be king over them all; they shall no longer be two nations, nor shall they ever be divided into two kingdoms again. 23 They shall not defile themselves anymore with their idols, nor with their detestable things, nor with any of their transgressions; but I will deliver them from all their dwelling places in which they have sinned, and will cleanse them. Then they shall be My*

---

[115] See Genesis 15 and 22

people, and I will be their Elohim." Ezekiel 37:21-23[116]

The Messiah came to renew the Covenant with Yisrael. He did not come to establish a new and different covenant with some fictitious entity called the Church.

This notion is mind boggling for most Christians who have been taught that Jesus did away with the Torah and started a new religion called Christianity that revolves around a new group of people called The Church. It is a foundational tenet of Christian doctrine, but it is simply not supported by the Scriptures when viewed in their original context and language.

Now if you are a Christian and feel defensive by this message do not fret. You need to step back, take a deep breath and relax. This book is not about attacking the Christian faith, rather it is all about restoring the truth of Yahushua's message. That message may be different from what you have been taught, but the Scriptures confirm everything contained in this discussion.

Therefore, if you truly desire to follow the Messiah you should be rejoicing. You have been provided with truth and clarity regarding these very difficult and confused issues. Now all you need to do from this point onward is to test whether your beliefs derive from the Scriptures or from tradition.

While the Christian religion recognizes that the Messiah came over two thousand years ago and died for our sins, it twists His teachings and distorts His identity. Essentially, the Christian religion has managed to morph the Messiah of Yisrael into a pagan christ that is diametrically opposed to the true Messiah.

---

[116] For a detailed discussion of the prophecies concerning the re-gathering and reuniting of the divided kingdom see the Walk in the Light series books entitled *The Redeemed* and *The Final Shofar*.

As a result, Christianity in all of its various forms actually promotes the very thing that the Messiah taught and warned against. Whether Christianity is actually a religion of Paul is subject to debate, what is not debatable is the fact that Christianity has become a religion that advocates lawlessness.

7

Lawlessness

The concept of lawlessness is described by a variety of terms in the Scriptures such as "iniquity" and "wickedness." While we often think of the word wicked applying to witches, warlocks, sorcerors and demons, in it's simplest sense, it means: "twisted." Just as the wick of a candle or lamp is twisted, when someone twists the truth they are deemed wicked.

So who are the wicked? We read in the Psalms that the wicked are those who forsake the Torah. "*Indignation has taken hold of me because of the wicked, who forsake Your Torah.*" (Psalm 119:53) So you don't have to be fully sold out to the dark side to be called wicked. You simply must forsake or reject the Torah.

In fact, wickedness is a snare that destroys. "*Keep me from the snares they have laid for me, and from the traps of the workers of iniquity.*" (Psalm 141:9) "*The cords of the wicked have bound me, but I have not forgotten Your Torah.*" Psalm 119:61. Wickedness is the opposite of the Torah. While Torah is the straight path, wickedness involves crookedness.

"*As for such as turn aside to their crooked ways,*
YHWH shall lead them away with the workers of iniquity.
Peace be upon Yisrael!"
Psalm 125:5

Notice that those with crooked ways are also called "workers of iniquity." YHWH hates the workers of iniquity[117] and He makes them depart from His presence.[118] The Hebrew word for "iniquity" is either "avone" (עונ) or "aven" (און). It refers to wickedness, vanity, idolatry and nothingness. So a worker of iniquity is a person who lives contrary to the ways of YHWH. They miss the mark and their works lead to nothing.

It is the opposite of the word for "righteous" which is "tsadik" (צדיק). The instructions in the Torah are "tsadik" (צדיק) and lead to righteousness – "tsadiqah" (צדקה). This was clearly set forth in the Scriptures. *"And what great nation is there that has such statutes and righteous judgments as are in all this Torah which I set before you this day?"* (Deuteronomy 4:8)

It is righteousness to walk according to the Torah. *"Then it will be righteousness for us, if we are careful to observe all these Commandments before YHWH our Elohim, as He has commanded us."* (Deuteronomy 6:25)

It is really that simple. Nothing has changed – not the definition of righteousness nor the way of righteousness. These cannot change because YHWH is righteous – "tsedeq" (צדיק)[119] and He does not change.[120]

So you do not have to be a satan worshipper to be wicked. You simply disobey the Commandments and refuse to walk in the way of righteousness. So wickedness is the opposite of righteousness and wickedness is lawlessness. Essentially the word "lawless" is "Torahless."

The wicked and the lawless are those who do not obey the Torah. Amazingly the Messiah predicted that there would be many who would call Him Lord who would actually be wicked.

---

[117] Psalm 5:5
[118] Psalm 6:8
[119] Exodus 9:27, 2 Chronicles 12:6, Psalms 11:7, 129:4 and 145:17, Lamentations 1:18, Zepheniah 3:5
[120] Malachi 3:6

"*²¹ Not everyone who says to Me, 'Lord, Lord,' shall enter the kingdom of heaven, but he who does the will of My Father in heaven. ²² Many will say to Me in that day, Lord, Lord, have we not prophesied in Your Name, cast out demons in Your name, and done many wonders in Your Name?' ²³ And then I will declare to them, 'I never knew you; depart from Me, you who practice lawlessness!'" (Matthew 7:21-23)

Those who practice lawlessness are the wicked, the worker's of iniquity. They reject the Torah. This is clear in the Greek text. The word for "lawlessness" is "anomia" (ἀνομία). It specifically means: "without the Torah." So the Messiah does not know the workers of lawlessness – those who live and do works contrary to the Torah.

How interesting that these workers of lawlessness are prophesying, casting out demons and doing many wonders. When I grew up in Christianity these were the people who I always thought were the powerful, spiritually anointed ones. Interestingly, the Messiah is not concerned about those works in and of themselves. Rather, He defines people by whether or not they obey the Torah.[121]

It is also interesting to note that these many claim to be calling on His Name, but He does not know them. It is quite possible that they do not actually know His Name. Thus is what Christians are doing when they

---

[121] This passage baffles many because they assume that people exercising spiritual power must be living and acting properly in the eyes of YHWH. This is clearly not the case as pointed out by the Messiah to His disciples. (see Mark 9:38-39 and Luke 9:49-50). YHWH desires people to be healed and freed from demonic depression and allows people to be freed through their faith, even if it is misplaced. Therefore, it is more about the ones being healed and freed than it is the one performing the miracles. That is why following signs and wonders alone can be deceptive and will, in fact, deceive many. Yahushua warned: "For false christs and false prophets will rise and show great signs and wonders to deceive, if possible, even the elect." Matthew 24:23 and Mark 13:22. The Book of Revelation, referring to the beast, warns as follows: "*¹³ He performs great signs, so that he even makes fire come down from heaven on the earth in the sight of men. ¹⁴ And he deceives those who dwell on the earth by those signs which he was granted to do in the sight of the beast, telling those who dwell on the earth to make an image to the beast who was wounded by the sword and lived." Revelation 13:13-14.

insist on calling the Messiah Jesus instead of His real Name Yahushua. In fact, there can be little doubt that Yahsuhua is referring to Christians in the passage. They are the only group of many people who claim to follow the Messiah but reject the Torah.

The only way that you can have a relationship with the Messiah is through His Covenant. When you enter into Covenant then He declares "I am your Elohim" and He calls you "My People." That is the Covenant language used throughout the Scriptures and in order to be in Covenant you must obey the terms of the Covenant – His Commandments.

The Covenant path is the narrow way and we are not to turn to the right or to the left, but rather walk the straight way. "[24] *Strive to enter through the narrow gate, for many, I say to you, will seek to enter and will not be able.* [25] *When once the Master of the house has risen up and shut the door, and you begin to stand outside and knock at the door, saying, "Lord, Lord, open for us,' and He will answer and say to you, 'I do not know you, where you are from,'* [26] *then you will begin to say, 'We ate and drank in Your presence, and You taught in our streets.'* [27] *But He will say, 'I tell you I do not know you, where you are from. Depart from Me, all you workers of iniquity.'* [28] *There will be weeping and gnashing of teeth, when you see Abraham and Isaac and Jacob and all the Prophets in the kingdom of Elohim, and yourselves thrust out.*" (Luke 13:24-28)

Again, the workers of iniquity are the lawless ones. They reject the Torah. Abraham, Isaac and Jacob are the fathers of the Covenant and they will be in the Kingdom because they are in the Covenant. The ones in the Kingdom are the ones in the Covenant – the ones who hear and obey (shema).

Yahushua drove the point home in His famous parable of the tares and the wheat.

"²⁴ The kingdom of heaven is like a man who sowed good seed in his field; ²⁵ but while men slept, his enemy came and sowed tares among the wheat and went his way. ²⁶ But when the grain had sprouted and produced a crop, then the tares also appeared. ²⁷ So the servants of the owner came and said to him, 'Sir, did you not sow good seed in your field? How then does it have tares?' ²⁸ He said to them, 'An enemy has done this.' The servants said to him, 'Do you want us then to go and gather them up?' ²⁹ But he said, 'No, lest while you gather up the tares you also uproot the wheat with them. ³⁰ Let both grow together until the harvest, and at the time of harvest I will say to the reapers, First gather together the tares and bind them in bundles to burn them, but gather the wheat into my barn.'"
Matthew 13:24-30

After giving this parable Yahushua then offered the following interpretation. "³⁷ He answered and said to them: "He who sows the good seed is the Son of Man. ³⁸ The field is the world, the good seeds are the sons of the Kingdom, but the tares are the sons of the wicked one. ³⁹ The enemy who sowed them is the devil, the harvest is the end of the age, and the reapers are the angels. ⁴⁰ Therefore as the tares are gathered and burned in the fire, so it will be at the end of this age. ⁴¹ The Son of Man will send out His angels, <u>and they will gather out of His Kingdom all things that offend, and those who practice lawlessness,</u> ⁴² and will cast them into the furnace of fire. There will be wailing and gnashing of teeth. ⁴³ Then the righteous will shine forth as the sun in the Kingdom of their Father. He who has ears to hear, let him hear!" (Matthew 13:37-43)

So there will be weeping and gnashing of teeth as people recognize that they were deceived and missed out on what they thought they had. Of course, this is not a problem exclusively attributed to Christianity. There were many Yisraelites in the past who fell under the same delusion.

The prophet Jeremiah spoke to the House of Judah after the Kingdom had been divided and the House of Yisrael, the Northern Kingdom, had already been removed by the Assyrians. Those remaining in the House of Judah, the Southern Kingdom, believed that because they had the Temple they were alright. They put their faith in a building and a religious system, rather then an obedient relationship with Elohim.

> "*¹ The word that came to Jeremiah from YHWH, saying, ² Stand in the gate of YHWH's house, and proclaim there this word, and say, Hear the word of YHWH, all you of Judah who enter in at these gates to worship YHWH! ³ Thus says YHWH of hosts, the Elohim of Yisrael: Amend your ways and your doings, and I will cause you to dwell in this place. ⁴ Do not trust in these lying words, saying, The Temple of YHWH, the Temple of YHWH, the Temple of YHWH are these. ⁵ For if you thoroughly amend your ways and your doings, if you thoroughly execute judgment between a man and his neighbor, ⁶ if you do not oppress the stranger, the fatherless, and the widow, and do not shed innocent blood in this place, or walk after other gods to your hurt, ⁷ then I will cause you to dwell in this place, in the Land that I gave to your fathers forever and ever. ⁸ Behold, you trust in lying words that cannot profit. ⁹ Will you steal, murder, commit adultery, swear falsely, burn incense to Baal, and walk after other gods whom you do not*

> know, ^{10} and then come and stand before Me in this House which is called by My Name, and say, 'We are delivered to do all these abominations? ^{11} Has this House, which is called by My Name, become a den of thieves in your eyes? Behold, I, even I, have seen it, says YHWH." Jeremiah 7:1-10

Sadly, they did not heed the warnings. They continued to operate in their artificial religious construct. It appeared as though they were serving YHWH, but they were lawless and their actions were abominable. They did not repent and obey. As a result, the Babylonians destroyed the Temple just as the Philistines had previously destroyed the Mishkan[122] in Shiloh.

Of course, Judah was permitted to return later and rebuild the Temple, but it was never fully restored. The Ark of the Covenant was not returned to the Temple and the Covenant was never fully restored. That would be the work left to the Messiah

He came with a message similar to Jeremiah's because the House of Judah had fallen into the same ways as their fathers. They had constructed a religious system around a Temple structure, but their hearts were not truly serving Elohim.

Yahushua came specifically stating: "It is written, 'My House is a House of Prayer,' but you have made it a 'den of thieves.'" (Luke 19:46) He also spoke specifically to the religious rulers. "^{27} Woe to you, scribes and Pharisees, hypocrites! For you are like whitewashed tombs which indeed appear beautiful outwardly, but inside are full of dead men's bones and all uncleanness. ^{28} Even so you also outwardly appear righteous to men, but inside you are full of hypocrisy and

---

[122] "Mishkan" is the term often used to describe the Tabernacle that was set up in Shiloh. It became more of a permanent structure during the centuries that it was located in the territory of Ephraim, prior to the permanent Temple being built in Jerusalem.

lawlessness." (Matthew 23:27-28)

The religion of Judaism has developed from those same Pharisees. Many mistakenly believe that Judaism is the same religion followed by ancient Yisrael but, as already mentioned, that is not the case. Judaism is Talmudism. It is a religion developed by the Pharisees after the destruction of the Temple in 70 CE, and it is based upon the traditions and the laws developed by the Pharisees. It is disconnected from Scriptural Yisrael and the Covenant renewed by Messiah.

That was the point that the Messiah repeatedly made when He rebuked them. It is a religion that is guided by the traditions and laws of men. Read the following confrontation, which clearly reveals the issue.

> "*⁵ Then the Pharisees and Scribes asked Him, 'Why do Your disciples not walk according to the tradition of the elders, but eat bread with unwashed hands?' ⁶ He answered and said to them, 'Well did Isaiah prophesy of you hypocrites, as it is written: This people honors Me with their lips, but their heart is far from Me. ⁷ And in vain they worship Me, Teaching as doctrines the commandments of men. ⁸ For laying aside the Commandment of Elohim, you hold the tradition of men - the washing of pitchers and cups, and many other such things you do. ⁹ He said to them, <u>All too well you reject the Commandment of Elohim, that you may keep your tradition.</u>'" Mark 7:5-9*

So the Pharisees had developed laws and traditions that they enforced like Commandments. In fact, while they observed their traditions they actually neglected and rejected the Comandments of Elohim.

According to Yahushua, these traditions and laws

place heavy burdens on men. "*¹ Then Yahushua spoke to the multitudes and to His disciples, ² saying: 'The Scribes and the Pharisees sit in Moses' seat. ³ Therefore whatever they tell you to observe, that observe and do, but do not do according to their works; for they say, and do not do. ⁴ For they bind heavy burdens, hard to bear, and lay them on men's shoulders; but they themselves will not move them with one of their fingers."* (Matthew 23:1-4)

They sat in Moses' seat, which was a special place in the Synagogue where the Torah of Moses was read. So Yahushua was instructing people to listen to the Pharisees when they read the Torah of Moses, but we are not to follow their example. Their works were the result of their laws and traditions, which placed heavy burdens upon people.

In response, Yahushua said to take His yoke. Of course, His yoke is the Torah. "*²⁹ Take My yoke upon you and learn from Me, for I am gentle and lowly in heart, and you will find rest for your souls. ³⁰ For My yoke is easy and My burden is light.*" (Matthew 11:29-30)

Most Christians incorrectly believe that obeying the Torah is legalism and that the Pharisees were legalistic because of their Torah observance. Not so. They added to and took away from the Torah, which was specifically prohibited.

> "You shall not add to the Word which I command you, nor take from it, that you may keep the Commandments of YHWH your Elohim which I command you."
> Deuteronomy 4:2

> "Do not add to His Words, lest He rebuke you, and you be found a liar."
> Proverbs 30:6

The Pharisees placed their traditions and their

man-made laws above the Torah, and as a result, they too were described as lawless.[123]

So both the religion of Christianity and Judaism are lawless religions. They have both neglected the Commandments, instead preferring their own laws, rules, regulationss and traditions.

As if it could not be any clearer John stated the following: "*Whoever commits sin also commits lawlessness, and sin is lawlessness.*" (1 John 3:4) Sin and lawlessness are the same. So when a person confesses that they are a sinner, they are confessing that they have not obeyed the Torah. They are confessing that they have been lawless.

Clearly, you do not get into the Kingdom if you are a lawless person.[124] In fact, when asked if only a few would be saved the Messiah answered in the affirmative. Here is the passage from Matthew:

> "*[13] Enter by the narrow gate; for wide is the gate and broad is the way that leads to destruction, and there are many who go in by it. [14] Because narrow is the gate and difficult is the way which leads to life, and there are few who find it.*" Matthew 7:13-14

---

[123] "*[27] Woe to you, scribes and Pharisees, hypocrites! For you are like whitewashed tombs which indeed appear beautiful outwardly, but inside are full of dead men's bones and all uncleanness. [28] Even so you also outwardly appear righteous to men, but inside you are full of hypocrisy and lawlessness.*" Matthew 23:27-28

[124] Yahushua made this very clear when He likened the Kingdom to a wedding feast. "*[11] But when the king came in to see the guests, he saw a man there who did not have on a wedding garment. [12] So he said to him, 'Friend, how did you come in here without a wedding garment?' And he was speechless. [13] Then the king said to the servants, 'Bind him hand and foot, take him away, and cast him into outer darkness; there will be weeping and gnashing of teeth.' [14] For many are called, but few are chosen.*" Matthew 22:11-14. It is very clear that those attending the wedding in the Kingdom must be clean "*not having spot or wrinkle or any such thing, but that she should be holy and without blemish.*" Ephesians 5:27. You must be cleansed by the blood of the Lamb to attend the Marriage Supper of the Lamb and, after receiving that cleansing, you must remain clean by living righteously. "*And to her it was granted to be arrayed in fine linen, clean and bright, for the fine linen is the righteous acts of the saints.*" Revelation 19:8. Righteous conduct is not something mysterious. It is defined in the Torah.

According to the Messiah many will try to get into the Kingdom, but the Master does not know them because they are defined as "workers of lawlessness."[125] They are the opposite of those who work righteousness.

Remember that righteousness and sin are defined through the Torah. Obedience is righteousness and disobedience is lawlessness. The workers of lawlessness are lawless individuals who have refused to take on the yoke of the Torah and labor for the Kingdom. They work iniquity instead of righteousness.

A popular focus in Christianity is that you need to know Jesus as "your personal Lord and Savior." It is critical to understand that our relationship status is provided through the Covenant.

Yahushua made it abundantly clear that our relationship is defined by our conduct, not simply a decision that we made at some point in our lives. And it is not the actions that we think we should do, but rather, what He commands us to do.

Those who refuse to do what He commands are defined as lawless, and the lawless ones do not get into the Kingdom - not even those who work miracles and claim to be prophets. They do not have a "personal relationship" with Him as Lord and Savior, even though they think they do.

Again, read those haunting words spoken by Yahushua: *"[15] Beware of false prophets, who come to you in sheep's clothing, but inwardly they are ravenous wolves. [16] You will know them by their fruits. Do men gather grapes from thorn bushes or figs from thistles? [17] Even so, every good tree bears good fruit, but a bad tree bears bad fruit. [18] A good tree cannot bear bad fruit, nor can a bad tree bear good fruit. [19]*

---

[125] Matthew 7:23

Every tree that does not bear good fruit is cut down and thrown into the fire. [20] Therefore by their fruits you will know them. [21] <u>Not everyone who says to Me, 'Lord, Lord,' shall enter the kingdom of heaven, but he who does the will of My Father in heaven. [22] Many will say to Me in that day, 'Lord, Lord, have we not prophesied in Your name, cast out demons in Your name, and done many wonders in Your name?' [23] And then I will declare to them, 'I never knew you; depart from Me, you who practice lawlessness!'"</u> Matthew 7:15-23

Those who practice lawlessness are those "without the Torah." They are the ones who do not follow the Commandments. He does not know those who do not follow His Commandments. In other words, He does not have a relationship with those people. It does not matter what you say or do if you are not bearing good fruit by obeying the Commandments.

The Commandments are at the heart of the Covenant and the Covenant defines the relationship between Elohim and mankind. You are not in a relationship with Him if you are not in Covenant with Him. As a result, if you think or state that you have a relationship with the Messiah outside the Covenant or the Commandments you are mistaken. You may find yourself in that group of "many" described by the Messiah.

If you think that you can just say a prayer and then disregard the Commandments then you are deceived. In fact, the Scriptures go so far as to call you a liar if you say such a thing. "*He who says, 'I know Him,' and does not keep His Commandments, is a liar, and the truth is not in him.*" (1 John 2:4) The standard for knowing Him is clear. "*Now by this we know that we know Him, if we keep His Commandments.*" (1 John 2:3)

This fact is made abundantly clear throughout the Scriptures. If you refuse to obey you do not get into the Kingdom. Further, if you are in the Kingdom and decide not to obey you get ejected from the Kingdom. That is exactly what happened to Adam and Eve[126] in the Garden of Eden. *"The Son of Man will send out His angels, and they will gather out of His Kingdom all things that offend, and those who practice lawlessness."* (Matthew 13:41)

These lawless ones likely started by loosening the Commandments, which ultimately led to them breaking the Commandments. They will not remain in the Kingdom. Thanks to Yahushua, there is forgiveness for sins through His shed blood. The symbolism of the blood on the doorposts and the mantel at Passover reveals that His blood make a way for us back into the Garden. That is why He stated: *"I am the door."*[127]

The entire goal of the Covenant, renewed through the blood of Yahushua, involves a return to the Garden where we find fellowship with our Creator – the source of life. The Hebrew word for "garden" is "gan" (גן) and it means "an enclosed or protected space." The Garden of Eden was hedged in by the Commandments.[128]

Sadly, most religions fail to understand or represent the principles of the Kingdom. This should be no surprise. The Messiah claimed that rampant lawlessness would be a sign of the end. *"And because lawlessness will abound, the love of many will grow cold."* (Matthew 24:12) Notice that lawlessness is directly linked with the lack of love for Elohim, and remember that love is directly connected with obedience.[129]

Our actions define and demonstrate our love or

---

[126] The actual Hebrew name of the woman commonly called Eve is "Hawah" (הוה). It means: "life giver."
[127] See John 10:7 and 10:9
[128] The Garden represented the Kingdom of YHWH. The Commandments are the rule of the Kingdom. That is why the man and the woman were expelled from the Kingdom. They "broke the law" and were punished by being exiled.
[129] John 14:15 and 15:10

lack thereof. There are many who claim to love God or Jesus, but their actions reveal who they are truly serving. If they reject the Torah and are living lives of lawlessness then they do not love Yahushua. They love themselves, their religion, their religious leaders or their traditions.

The Messiah specifically said: "*²³ If anyone loves Me, he will keep My word; and My Father will love him, and We will come to him and make Our home with him. ²⁴ He who does not love Me does not keep My words; and the word which you hear is not Mine but the Father's who sent Me.*" (John 14:23-24)

There is no difference - the Word of Yahushua is the same as the Word of YHWH. The Commandments of Yahushua are the same as the Commandments of YHWH. There is no distinction or disparity between the two. Yahushua said ". . . he who has seen me has seen the Father . . ." John 14:9. He also said: "I and the Father are one." (John 10:30) He was the Word from the beginning[130] and He never changed the Torah by fulfilling the prophecies and renewing the Covenant.

Thus, as people increasingly reject His Word (the Torah), their love grows cold. As they continue in lawlessness, they stray farther and farther from Him. The Commandments are like a gentle yoke. They steer and guide us in the right direction. When our lives are guided by the Commandments, we will be productive servants, plowing the fallow ground so that the seeds of the Kingdom can be planted and the Kingdom can grow and bear fruit through the righteous ones.

If we refuse to go the way of the Commandments, but instead choose our own path, we will be of no use to the King. We will be cut off and

---

[130] See John 1

thrown into the fire.[131] This is what Yahushua said so you should not be shocked by this message. This is exactly what He was referring to when He rejected the lawless ones. They are *many* who are doing what they want instead of what He commands. There is no denying that this group of *many* people sounds exactly like the modern Christian Church. In fact, there really is no other group of people on Earth that fits the description.

Those in the Christian religion specifically claim to follow the Messiah, but many do not really know Him. They do not even know His Name. They certainly do not love Him if they refuse to obey His Commandments. Many are serving a fictional christ that advocates lawlessness. They also rely on an erroneous understanding of "grace" for salvation while rejecting and neglecting the terms of the Covenant that provides salvation and deliverance.[132]

The Messiah was very clear when He stated: *"²⁹ Take My yoke upon you and learn from Me, for I am gentle and lowly in heart, and you will find rest for your souls. ³⁰ For My yoke is easy and My burden is light."* Matthew 11:29-30

Sadly, most Christians interpret this passage to mean that the yoke of the Torah was too difficult for men to bear, as if the Father is a cruel slave driver, placing a burden upon Yisrael that was too heavy to bear. So cruel was the Father that the Son had to come

---

[131] See John 15:5-8

[132] There is a popular teaching in Christianity that promotes the notion that grace has replaced the Torah. This largely derives from statements from Paul such as: "For sin shall not have dominion over you, for you are not under law but under grace." Romans 6:14. Of course, there is no possible way that a statement from Paul could diminish the importance of the Torah in any way. Grace is the favor given to us through the Messiah. It is the free gift of atonement that we receive through His shed blood. We need the forgiveness because we have violated the Torah. Once we receive the forgiveness we should seek to live in obedience to the Commandments. This is not so we can earn salvation. It is merely our expression of love and thanksgiving to Elohim.

and remove that burden and give us a lighter one. This is a twisted and perverted understanding of Elohim. It infiltrated Christianity through an ancient heretic named Marcion in the second century.[133]

His yoke was always easy. In fact, He is the one who delivers His people from bondage and slavery. He relieves His people from the heavy yoke of the slavemaster and the burdens that religions and the traditions of men place upon us. In the passage in Matthew 11, Yahushua was referring specifically to Hosea 11. It describes how YHWH gently guided Yisrael, as a father would a child.

"*¹ When Yisrael was a child, I loved him, and out of Egypt I called My son. ² As they called them, so they went from them; They sacrificed to the Baals, and burned incense to carved images. ³ I taught Ephraim to walk, taking them by their arms; but they did not know that I healed them. ⁴ I drew them with gentle cords, with bands of love, and I was to them as those who take the yoke from their neck. I stooped and fed them.*" Hosea 11:1-4

Ephraim was the leading tribe from the House of Yisrael and therefore often represented the House of Yisrael after the Kingdom was divided. The Creator does not oppress us with a heavy burden. Rather, He gently guides us. Notice the tenderness that YHWH demonstrated to His children. He lovingly directs us to Him.

The difficulty comes when we are surrounded

---

[133] Marcion of Sinope lived between 85 CE and 160 CE. He was the Bishop of a heretical religious sect referred to as the Marcionites. He taught a dualist belief system that the god of the Old Testament was a separate and distinct god from the New Testament. As a result, he emphasized various texts over the Old Testament and essentially threw out the foundation of the faith. Because of the destructive nature of his false teachings, many attribute the decision to develop the canon of the New Testament to Marcion. The development of the canon of the New Testament was essentially an attempt to solidify orthodox doctrine and agree upon texts that supported that doctrine. Prior to that time, various letters and Gospels were circulating amongst the Assemblies, and were not treated as Scriptures.

by the nations and drawn to their false gods and idols. We also get burdened by laws, rules, regulations and traditions heaped upon us by religions. The Commandments themselves are certainly not too difficult to obey. In fact, it is the Commandments that provide rest.[134]

Recall that this was specifically stated by Moses after he spoke the words of the Covenant before the people entered into the Promised Land. *"For this Commandment which I command you today is not too mysterious for you, nor is it far off."* Deuteronomy 30:11

Some translations state: *"it is not too difficult."* In other words, it can be known and it can be done. He isn't saying that it won't be difficult, just not too difficult.

Remember that this was also specifically stated in the New Testament. *"For this is the love of Elohim, that we keep His Commandments. And His Commandments are not burdensome."* (1 John 5:3)

So how can so many people be deceived in the end? The answer, in large part, rests on their misunderstanding of what it means to love Elohim.

---

[134] The Commandments provide a day of rest every week. The seventh day, known as the Sabbath, is an incredible gift discussed further in the Walk in the Light series book entitled *The Sabbath*. We are also provided rest days known as "shabbaton," which fall on various Appointed Times. Those shabbaton are discussed further in the Walk in the Light series book entitled *Appointed Times*.

8

All You Need Is Love

One of the major arguments that Christians will pose against keeping the Commandments is that Jesus taught love. They believe that he freed us from the Law and now all we have to do is love.

Of course, we already saw the absurdity of that argument because the Torah was given as an expression of love, and only through the Torah can you find true freedom. If you are not living according to the righteous instructions of the Torah you are in bondage. You are a slave to sin and under a curse of separation from Elohim that leads to death.

This understanding is a critical paradigm shift that every Christian must make in order to recognize what Yahushua actually taught.

He did teach love, but love centered in the Commandments. He taught the greatest Commandment was to love YHWH *"with all your heart, with all your soul and with all your mind"*[135] and *"with all your heart, with all your soul, with all your mind and with all your strength."*[136]

Recall that this is the Shema and there is an incredible mystery in the Hebrew text of the Shema involving the Messiah. Read it again and see what is hidden from the English translation.

"4 Hear, O Yisrael: YHWH our Elohim, YHWH is one!

---

[135] Matthew 22:37
[136] Mark 12:30

⁵ You shall love את YHWH your Elohim with all your heart, with all your soul, and with all your strength."
Deuteronomy 6:4-5

Did you notice the Aleph Taw (את) in between YHWH and love? This reveals that the Messiah is the ultimate expression of how we love YHWH. So we listen, learn and follow Yahushua as He teaches us how to love Elohim. He says that the Shema is the greatest of the Commandments and the word "shema" means to hear and obey. It is clearly focused on the Commandments and the Commandments are how we love YHWH with all our heart, all our soul and all our strength.

In fact the next four verses of the Shema clearly make that point: "*⁶ <u>And these Words which I command you today shall be in your heart.</u> ⁷ You shall teach them diligently to your children, and shall talk of them when you sit in your house, when you walk by the way, when you lie down, and when you rise up. ⁸ You shall bind them as a sign on your hand, and they shall be as frontlets between your eyes. ⁹ You shall write them on the doorposts of your house and on your gates.*" (Deuteronomy 6:6-9)

So, the Commandments are supposed to be in our hearts. Only when they are inside our hearts can we truly obey **with all of our heart**. Then we focus on the Commandments with all our soul – our being. We think and meditate upon them and we speak of them. We diligently obey them with all our strength and when we understand how to obey them we diligently teach them to our children. We bind them to ourselves so that they control everything that we do, and we write them on our doorposts and gates as a reminder that they rule our homes.

This is clearly not just an emotional response or a feeling - it is a way of life. It reveals the difference between western thinking and eastern thinking. Western thought places love in the ethereal realm of feelings and emotions. In western thought, love is a very abstract notion and when you ask a westerner to define love they will typically mention feelings.

This is a problem with western civilization. It has become a culture largely focused on appetite and emotions. As a result, love is based primarily on an emotional response and that emotion involves a feeling. It is a good feeling and therefore love becomes primarily focused on the person experiencing the emotion, not the other person in the relationship. As long as you feel good around the other person then you continue to love them. When you stop feeling good or the feelings dissipate, you "fall out of love."

That's not love. That's simply selfish and that is the problem with defining love as an emotion. All you have to do is view the divorce rates and the failure of marriages in modern western societies to discern that there is a serious misunderstanding of love.

Amazingly, the divorce rates among Christians are essentially the same as the divorce rates of secular society, which reveals that Christianity shares the same selfish and distorted notion of love as society in general. In fact, since Christianity has been the religion that has influenced western society the most, one could argue that Christianity is responsible for this epidemic societal failure.

Now here is the real shocker - Christians actually have the audacity to believe that they are The Bride of Christ. The problem is that many do not even know how to love their own spouses, and because of erroneous doctrines many clearly do not know how to love Yahushua. That is likely why half of those who are seeking to be wedded to the Bridegroom will miss out on the Great Wedding Feast according to the parable of the

Ten Virgins. Only half of them are prepared for that great event.[137]

The Christian Church is not the Bride of the Messiah because she has strayed from the righteous path. The Christian Church has adopted the ways of Babylon and is more aptly described as the Daughter of Babylon rather than the Daughter of Zion. This is evident in modern western Christianity, which focuses on building large structures to attract great numbers through worship services that better resemble concerts. People are often searching for an experience and they confuse an emotional high with being filled with the Spirit.

Modern church services have become entertainment driven and the sermons are generally focused on motivating the congregants toward positive thinking and prosperity. The point is to have congregants who feel good about themselves and their lives. Modern Christianity is often catering to the love of self rather than than the love of Elohim, and it is the perfect religion for selfish, greedy, entertainment and consumer driven western cultures.

Indeed, most people become Christians so they can get something – eternal life. If it were not for that irresistible free offer, or being scared to death of going to hell, it is doubtful whether many would ever convert. So from the beginning, many Christians are driven primarily by emotions.

Now that is not to say that emotions do not play a part in love. Of course they do. They are built into the very fabric of our being. The only problem is that they cannot be the only component of love, otherwise our concept of love becomes distorted.

There are also different ways of expressing love, depending upon the specific relationship. Clearly, husbands and wives convey their love for one another in

---

[137] See the parable of the 10 Virgins at Matthew 25:1-13.

a uniquely intimate fashion. It differs from how they love their children, their parents, their siblings and their friends. Every role has its own unique form of love. We instinctively know how to love our family and the Scriptures provide specific guidance on relationships outside the family unit - our Elohim and our neighbors.

The Scriptures reveal that we express our love for Elohim by obeying His Commandments - that is the Shema. We also are instructed to love our neighbor as we love ourselves. The second most important Commandment, according to the Messiah, involves love and it essentially deals with everyone that we relate with outside of our home.

Of course, that Commandment acknowledges the fact that we are all wired to take care of ourselves. We are all selfish, but that needs to be tempered and controlled. The Commandment to love your neighbor as yourself in Leviticus 19:18 reminds us that we should not simply be focused on our own needs, but also the needs of others.

Now it is easy to love a neighbor who mows our lawn, watches our house when we are on vacation and invites us over for barbeques, but Yahushua taught the Commandment as it was intended to be observed. When asked the question: "who is my neighbor?" He answered with the parable of the Good Samaritan.

> "*30 A certain man went down from Jerusalem to Jericho, and fell among thieves, who stripped him of his clothing, wounded him, and departed, leaving him half dead. 31 Now by chance a certain priest came down that road. And when he saw him, he passed by on the other side. 32 Likewise a Levite, when he arrived at the place, came and looked, and passed by on the other side. 33 But a certain Samaritan, as he*

journeyed, came where he was. And when he saw him, he had compassion. ³⁴ So he went to him and bandaged his wounds, pouring on oil and wine; and he set him on his own animal, brought him to an inn, and took care of him. ³⁵ On the next day, when he departed, he took out two denarii, gave them to the innkeeper, and said to him, "Take care of him; and whatever more you spend, when I come again, I will repay you.' ³⁶ So which of these three do you think was neighbor to him who fell among the thieves?"
Luke 10:30-36

So the answer to the question: Who is my neighbor?" was "*He who showed mercy on him.*" The Samaritan was on a journey. He clearly did not live next door to the man from Jerusalem who was injured. Samaritans did not live in Jerusalem, they lived in Samaria and worshipped on Mount Gerezim.

The implication is that the injured person was a Yisraelite because he came from Jerusalem. The Cohen and Priest who passed him were also Yisraelites, so they would clearly be considered to be his neighbor.

The Samaritan was a stranger and it is also important to understand that the Samaritans were despised by the Jews. While the Samaritans actually followed the Torah to a certain extent, they had a Temple on Mount Gerazim and they were separated from the Jews.[138]

So your neighbor is anyone of your fellow man

---

[138] The Samaritans used certain altered texts but generally followed the Torah. The main difference was the location of their Temple - Mount Gerazim. The reason it was not in Jerusalem was because they were originally not from the region of Samaria or the Land of Yisrael. They were foreigners transplanted there by the Assyrians after the House of Yisrael had been exiled and completely removed from their land. The Samaritans were generally taught the ways of YHWH, but that also ended up being mixed worship. The removal of the House of Yisrael and their replacement can be read in 2 Kings 17.

who is in need, whether a native born or an alien. Of course, this was not a new teaching. It was a teaching straight from the Torah. The Yisraelites were always instructed to love the stranger.

"*The stranger (alien) who dwells among you shall be to you as one born among you, and <u>you shall love him as yourself</u>; for you were strangers in the land of Egypt: I am YHWH your Elohim.*" (Leviticus 19:34)

Again, Yahushua was teaching the heart of the Torah to Yisraelites. That is what He was doing when He taught what is commonly referred to as the Golden Rule. Here is the passage: "*Therefore, whatever you want men to do to you, do also to them, for this is the Torah and the Prophets.*" (Matthew 7:12) Did you catch the last part? He was not issuing a new Commandment. He was distilling the essence of the Torah and revealing what the Torah and the Prophets taught.

So He always focused people toward the fact that love was at the heart of the Commandments, but that does not mean He did away with the Commandments. Remember that the Commandments were given out of love.

Some mistranslate a passage to support the idea that He did away with all of the Torah and provided only one new replacement Commandment. Here is that passage: "*A new commandment I give to you, that you love one another; as I have loved you, that you also love one another.*" (John 13:34)

There are those who think this means that Yahushua gave a brand new commandment just to love. We have already seen that this is not the case. The word for "new" in the text is "kainos" (καινός) in the Greek, and that word refers to renewing or refreshing.

Yahushua was simply saying that He showed His disciples how to love according to the Torah. He lived out that love in their presence, and now they were supposed to emulate that love in their lives. He is also likely emphasizing that it is like a new commandment because they hadn't been observing it.

This was reiterated by John: "*And now I plead with you . . . not as though I wrote a new commandment to you, but that which we have had from the beginning: that we love one another.*" (2 John 5) John was clearly saying that there was nothing new at all about loving one another. That was always the case from the beginning.

So the notion of love, and even the Commandment to love, was nothing new presented by Yahushua. He showed us how to love and that is how He fulfilled the Torah. Sadly, this has been misunderstood and twisted to support the notion that followers of Yahushua only need to love, and they do not have to obey the Commandments.

While love eminates from within, it is not centered primarily upon internal emotions and feelings, but rather on our response to those emotions. Indeed, the Christian response stands in direct opposition to the Pharisaic focus on external conduct. In reality we need both. As we saw in the parable of the Good Samaritan, his actions evidenced the fact that he loved his neighbor.

Yahushua focused on circumcised hearts first. The Pharisees focused on circumcised flesh. Yahushua was prioritizing not destroying. He was showing that love is at the heart of the Torah. It flows from the heart outward.

So how do we love Elohim? Quite simply, by keeping His Commandments. Again, Yahushua specifically stated "*If you keep My Commandments, you will abide in My love, just as I have kept My Father's Commandments and abide in His love.*" (John 15:10)

You cannot just feel love - you must live it. You cannot just believe in God, you must express your love through obedience. Sadly, many have confused the notion of obedience as an expression of love with obedience as a way of earning salvation.

They equate obedience with legalism and striving to earn your way into heaven through self-righteous conduct. You cannot earn your salvation through obedience. That is not the point of our obedience. When we love Him we trust Him to save us. That is faith.

We obey Him because we love Him. Love and obedience are always linked together. Consider the promise of the Second of the Ten Commandments: "... *but showing mercy to thousands, to those who love Me <u>and</u> keep My Commandments.*"[139]

If we trust Him and obey Him, He will love us in return. "*He who has My Commandments and keeps them, it is he who loves Me. And he who loves Me will be loved by My Father, and I will love him and manifest Myself to him.*" (John 14:21)

If we refuse to obey Him and continue to live in lawlessness then we are demonstrating that we do not really love Him.

Sadly, the Christian religion, through tradition, results in Christians living in lawlessness, which means that they do not love Him. This fact should shock every Christian and compel them to consider this difficult conundrum.

---

[139] Exodus 20:6

9

The Conundrum

It should be clear by now that the Messiah obeyed, taught and lived the Torah. Indeed He was the Torah in the flesh. It should also be clear that YHWH is in the process of establishing His Kingdom through His Son and the Bride Yisrael. This will restore what was lost in the Garden. He is building a House and filling that House with a Covenant family. After the fall and expulsion from the Garden, the door to the House was slammed shut. The Messiah has now opened that door for those who choose to obey.

YHWH explains in His Torah how He desires to be worshipped. He specifically commands His people not to worship Him as the pagans worship their gods.[140] This is particularly egregious when Christians choose pagan times over the Appointed Times of YHWH. These are rooted in Babylonian sun worship and that is why YHWH exhorts His people to come out of Babylon.[141]

There was actually a pattern for exiting Babylon established and demonstrated through the life of a man named Abram. Abram was uncircumcised when He was called by YHWH. This is a condition likened to the nations of the world that were disbursed from Babylon after the Tower of Babel event.

Abram believed the promise of YHWH and he acted. In fact, his actions defined his relationship with YHWH and were the proof of his belief. That belief, demonstrated by his actions, was accounted to him as

---

[140] Deuteronomy 12:30-31
[141] Revelation 18:4

righteousness.¹⁴² He crossed over into the Promised Land. This is the source of the word "Hebrew." It is "eber" (עבר) in the Hebrew language and it means "to cross over."

The word "Hebrew" refers to all those who believe the promises of YHWH, exit Babylon by "crossing over through the waters of immersion" and inherit the Promised Land through a Covenant relationship.¹⁴³ That Covenant was the path that YHWH established for mankind to return to Him.

The Land represented a restoration to the Garden of Eden, only this time it would be populated by a group of people brought out of Babylon who were committed to obeying the Commandments of Elohim. These people would enter into a Covenant of Marriage with YHWH.

After leaving Babylon, the uncircumcised Abram entered into a blood Covenant relationship with YHWH. Through that Covenant, YHWH demonstrated that He would provide the "atonement" and incur the penalty for breaking the Covenant.¹⁴⁴ Abram was also promised a great number of descendants and land for those descendants. This would be the path of restoration for mankind. The only way that mankind could dwell with YHWH was through a process of cleansing and restoring him to righteousness.

Later, when he progressed into the Covenant of Circumcision, Abram (אברם) received the new name – Abraham (אברהם). His wife Sarai (שרי) also received the new name – Sarah (שרה). They both had the letter "hey" (ה) added to their original names. The Hebrew letter

---

¹⁴² Genesis 15:6
¹⁴³ There were no bridges in those days. If you wanted to cross over a river it involved getting wet. This is why those who enter into the Covenant get baptized, or immersed. We get cleansed in preparation for our dwelling with a "holy" Elohim. It is symbolic of the complete cleansing that we receive when we are washed by the blood of the Lamb of Elohim.
¹⁴⁴ Genesis 15

"hey" (ה) often represents the "breath or the spirit," and adding a "hey" (ה) to the names of these two individuals represents the fact that the Covenant involves being transformed by the Spirit of YHWH.[145]

The point of that Covenant was to reveal that the Kingdom would be established through the seed of Abraham - renewed beings circumcised in the flesh and in the hearts and filled with the Spirit of Elohim. This was a family affair and anyone was welcome to join into the Covenant. By entering into the Covenant, they joined the Covenant family.

That Covenant extended through the descendants of Abraham, Isaac and the 12 sons of Jacob, who was renamed Yisrael. The 12 tribes eventually grew into a nation while enslaved in Egypt. Known collectively as the Children of Yisrael they were delivered from Egypt in a miraculous fashion so that the world would know the Name of YHWH.[146]

They were delivered along with a mixed multitude of people.[147] The point was clear, YHWH wanted the Nations to join into His Covenant through the Covenant established with Yisrael. In fact, He specifically stated that there was one Torah for the native Yisraelite and all the strangers who dwelled with them.[148]

This is a concept lost in time as the Kingdom of Yisrael fragmented and divided into two separate kingdoms. Accordingly, it is important to understand history in order to place the Scriptures within their original context. As we have already seen, language is also important.

---

[145] It is important to recognize that the Name of YHWH (יהוה) in Hebrew includes two "heys" (ה) joined together by a "vav" (ו). The vav is the sixth letter in the Hebrew alephbet and represents man.
[146] Exodus 9:16
[147] Exodus 12:38
[148] Exodus 12:49; Numbers 15:16

For instance, Yisrael (יִשְׂרָאֵל) is often translated to mean "He has striven with El."[149] We know the word "El" (אֵל) refers to Elohim, but what many have failed to recognize is that at the heart of the word Yisrael is "sar" (שַׂר), which means: "prince" or "royalty."[150] So these people were meant to be a royal assembly brought into relationship with YHWH through the Covenant.

In fact, after being brought out of Egypt, these people participated in a Marriage Covenant with YHWH at Mount Sinai. This assembly, collectively called Yisrael, became the Bride of YHWH. They were given the Torah as a "ketubah" (כְּתוּבָה), also known as a marriage contract. It set forth the terms of the relationship.

Yisrael was supposed to move into the marital residence, which was the Promised Land. Sadly, they feared the inhabitants of the Land, namely the giants, and refused to enter in. It is important to understand what was going on here. YHWH previously wiped out

---

[149] This translation is based upon the event where Jacob wrestled with a "Man" until the break of day. The "Man" did not prevail and stated: "Your name shall no longer be called Jacob, but אֵם-Yisrael; for you have struggled with אֵם -Elohim and with אֵם -men, and have prevailed." (Genesis 32:28) There is an amazing word play found in the Hebrew text and I have provided some of those mysteries in the translated text. The word "em" (אֵם) means: "mother" while the word "am" (עַם) means: "people or assembly." So while Jacob's name was being changed, we can see that this Yisrael would be the womb that would give birth to an Assembly of men who would be an assembly of Elohim.

[150] This fact was clearly revealed when YHWH stated: "And you shall be to Me a kingdom of priests and a holy nation. These are the words which you shall speak to the children of Yisrael." (Exodus 19:6) This was the heart of the Covenant made with Abram and Sarai when their names were changed to Abraham and Sarah. "I will make you exceedingly fruitful; and I will make nations of you, and kings shall come from you." (Genesis 17:6) "And I will bless her and also give you a son by her; then I will bless her, and she shall be a mother of nations; kings of peoples shall be from her." (Genesis 17:16) This was later confirmed to the man newly named Yisrael. "¹⁰ And Elohim said to him, 'Your name is Jacob; your name shall not be called Jacob anymore, but Yisrael shall be your name.' So He called his name Yisrael. " Also Elohim said to him: 'I am Elohim Almighty. Be fruitful and multiply; a nation and a company of nations shall proceed from you, and kings shall come from your body.'" (Genesis 35:10-11)

the Nephilim offspring[151] through a flood. The Nephilim continued their corruption of creation and actually littered the Promised Land with their offspring, which were an abomination in the eyes of YHWH. Their DNA was mixed with the Nephilim, which was a defilement of mankind - the image of Elohim.

This was a direct affront to YHWH and He intended to cleanse the Land with His new Bride, but she refused. He had already revealed His Mighty Hand by delivering her from bondage in Egypt, and was prepared to do the same as she entered into the Promised Land. Her response was a slap in the face to YHWH. After having previously broken the Covenant by committing idolatry with the Egyptian gods, represented by the golden calf, Yisrael was once again betraying her Husband.

YHWH would therefore wait for the next generation to enter in. Under the leadership of Joshua, better known as Yahushua, Yisrael eventually entered in and took the Land.[152] After the passage of hundreds of years YHWH gave Yisrael a king. The first king named Saul[153] did not diligently obey the Commandments of YHWH. The reign was therefore removed from him and given to David, the son of Jesse. David first ruled over the House of Judah for seven years. He was later annointed by the House of Yisrael and ruled over a united kingdom for thirty-three years. He reigned forty years in all.

After the death of King David, his son Solomon

---

[151] The Nephillim were fallen angels who actually bred with "the daughters of men." That resulted in a race of hybrid beings often referred to as "giants." This was described very briefly in Genesis 6:1-4. This was also described in the Book of Enoch.

[152] It is no coincidence that the leader who began as a servant of Mosheh and transformed into a conquering leader would be named Yahushua, the same name as the Messiah. This was a pattern that we would see fulfilled as he brought the Children of Yisrael across the Jordan as a corporate immersion and then circumcised them before he utterly destroyed the moon worshipping city of Jericho. This is a pattern that the Messiah will likely repeat in the future.

[153] It must be pointed out the Saul is also the name of the one commonly called Paul.

assumed the throne. While Solomon is often remembered for the wisdom bestowed upon him, his life ended miserably. He violated the Torah and participated in the worst forms of idolatry. As a result, the Kingdom would be divided between the north and the south. For the sake of David, his offspring would retain a portion of the Kingdom known as the House of Judah.

The Covenant people were originally collectively called Yisrael, but after they were divided that name was attributed to the 10 tribes ruled by Ephraim.[154] They were called the House of Yisrael, or the Northern Kingdom. The remaining tribes were ruled by Judah, known as the House of Judah, or the Southern Kingdom.

After separating, these two kingdoms individually rebelled and were exiled from the Promised Land. They both broke the Covenant and that Covenant needed to be restored with both Houses.

YHWH sent prophets to both Houses and promised a restoration. The House of Judah had been exiled by the Babylonians for 70 years, but only some returned at the end of the exile. She was never fully restored as a sovereign nation led by the seed of David.

The House of Yisrael had been divorced,[155] exiled by the Assyrians and scattered throughout the world. They needed a wedding in order to be restored to Him, and this was the context of and purpose of the Messiah. He would seek out the lost sheep of the House of Yisrael[156] and renew the Covenant with both Houses.[157]

This is precisely why YHWH sent His Son to die as the Lamb of Elohim in a specific place and at a specific time. If He were finished with Yisrael, He certainly would not have come for them and renewed the ancient Covenant at Passover with twelve disciples,

---

[154] See 1 Kings 12:20
[155] See Jeremiah 3:8
[156] See Matthew 10:6 and 15:24 in the context of Jeremiah 50.
[157] Jeremiah 31:31-32

representing all of the Tribes of Yisrael.

He was demonstrating that His blood would soon make the way for mankind to enter the House through the renewed Covenant with Yisrael. That is why He stated: *"Behold I stand at the door and knock. If anyone hears My voice and opens the door, I will come in to him and eat with him, and he with Me."*[158] This is all about a Covenant and a Covenant is sealed with a meal.

The Covenant begins at the door and is consummated through a meal, which is the result of the shed blood of the Covenant. This is the point of the Passover. It was a traditional blood covenant ritual that began at the threshold of the Yisraelite houses in Egypt and continued to the House of YHWH in the Promised Land.

As we can discern from the progression of the Appointed Times throughout the year, the Passover was only the beginning.[159] It marked the starting point for the Covenant journey.

Mankind needs to be cleansed and renewed. They need to have hearts to obey. Simply put, they need to have their hearts circumcised. This was always the focus of the Torah.[160] If you want to live in the House, you need to learn the rules of the House. If you ignore those rules then you will not be permitted in the House. It is really that simple.

Those who believe that they can receive the grace

---

[158] Revelation 3:20
[159] The Appointed Times are mentioned throughout the Torah, but the primary passage is found in Leviticus 23. It is there that we see the Appointed Times described by YHWH as *"My Appointed Times."* We also see the Covenant path laid out through these yearly rehearsals. It begins with the Passover meal, followed by a seven day Feast called the Feast of Unleavened Bread. After 50 days the Feast of Shabuot is celebrated, which is the culmination of the grain harvest. Also known as "firstfruits," it is the time when people bring their firstfruits from all over the Land to the House of YHWH. Then in the Seventh Month there is the Feast of Trumpets, followed by Yom Kippur, Succot and Shemini Atzeret. These all have a specific purpose and lead the Covenant people on the path to restoration. For a more detailed discussion of the Appointed Times see the Walk in the Light series book entitled *Appointed Times*.
[160] See Deuteronomy 10:16, 30:6, Jeremiah 4:4 and Ezekiel 36:26

of Elohim, be cleansed by the blood of Messiah and then live lives of sin and lawlessness are sadly mistaken. In fact, this will result in punishment of the highest order rendered upon those who have "*trampled the Son of Elohim underfoot, counted the blood of the Covenant by which He was sanctified a common thing, and insulted the Spirit of grace.*"[161]

This is just as true in the end as it was in the beginning. YHWH does not change.[162] He has declared the end from the very beginning. Hear the words of YHWH spoken through the Prophet Isaiah:

> "*9 Remember the former things of old, for I am Elohim, and there is no other; I am Elohim, and there is none like Me, 10 Declaring the end from the beginning, and from ancient times things that are not yet done, Saying, 'My counsel shall stand, and I will do all My pleasure,' 11 Calling a bird of prey from the east, the man who executes My counsel, from a far country. Indeed I have spoken it; I will also bring it to pass. I have purposed it; I will also do it. 12 Listen to Me, you stubborn-hearted, who are far from righteousness: 13 I bring My righteousness near, it shall not be far off; My salvation shall not linger. And I will place salvation in Zion, for Yisrael My glory.*" Isaiah 46:9-13

Just as we saw the Messiah in the beginning, the Word represented by the Aleph Taw (את), we also see Him in the end. There is a perfect continuity and flow in the Scriptures that is only understood when viewed from a Hebraic perspective. Yisrael is the glory of YHWH and Yisrael will be the Bride in the end.[163]

---

[161] Hebrews 10:29
[162] Malachi 3:6
[163] Clearly, we are not talking about the Modern State of Israel, which does not currently recognize the Messiah or follow the Torah. While many citizens in the

In fact, due to translation issues many people miss the connection specifically made by Yahushua. In the mysterious Book of Revelation, most English translations describe Yahushua as stating that He is "the Alpha and the Omega."[164] What they fail to recognize is that He is a Hebrew Messiah speaking to a Hebrew disciple. He would have been speaking in the Hebrew language.

Alpha (A) is the first letter in the Greek alphabet and Omega (Ω) is the last letter in the Greek alphabet. Since He was not speaking Greek, we understand that He did not refer to Himself as the Alpha and the Omega (AΩ), but rather, the Aleph Taw (את). So here we have a declaration from Yahushua that He is the Light and the Word from the beginning. He will come again in the end. Many will be unprepared for His coming because they have been taught lies and they do not know Him.

This was specifically revealed by Yahushua in the parable of the 10 virgins. "*¹ Then the kingdom of heaven shall be likened to ten virgins who took their lamps and went out to meet the bridegroom. ² Now five of them were wise, and five were foolish. ³ Those who were foolish took their lamps and took no oil with them, ⁴ but the wise took oil in their vessels with their lamps. ⁵ But while the bridegroom was delayed, they all slumbered and slept. ⁶ And at midnight a cry was heard: Behold, the bridegroom is coming; go out to meet him! ⁷ Then all those virgins arose and trimmed their lamps. ⁸ And the foolish said to the wise, Give us some of your oil, for our lamps are going out. ⁹ But the wise answered, saying, No, lest there should not be enough for us and you; but go rather to those who sell, and buy for yourselves. ¹⁰ And while they went to buy, the bridegroom came, and those who were ready went in with him*

---

modern state may join in the Covenant and become part of the Yisrael of YHWH, the two are not the same. This has caused great confusion, especially involving the prophecies, as people attempt to apply the prophecies concerning the Covenant Assembly of Yisrael to the modern State of Israel.

[164] Revelation 1:8, 1:11, 21:6, 22:13

to the wedding; and the door was shut. *¹¹ Afterward the other virgins came also, saying, Lord, Lord, open to us! ¹² But he answered and said, Assuredly, I say to you, I do not know you."* Matthew 25:1-12

Notice that all 10 were virgins and wanted to be with the Bridegroom. Only 5 were considered wise while the remaining 5 were foolish. All fell asleep, but the 5 wise were ready when the call was sounded. The foolish virgins were unprepared and ended up being shut out of the wedding feast. They did not properly discern the times and their lack of knowledge and preparedness had devastating consequences.

YHWH declared through the Prophet Hosea: *"My people are destroyed for lack of knowledge. Because you have rejected knowledge I also will reject you from being priest for Me. Because you have forgotten the Torah of your Elohim, I also will forget your children."* (Hosea 4:6)

We are currently living in a time when many of the called are sleeping. They lack knowledge and they have forgotten the Torah. They are unaware of the Appointed Times of YHWH and, therefore, they will be unprepared when the Messiah returns. As we approach the end of the age you must ask yourself whether you will be grouped with the wise or the foolish virgins? Will you be ready for the wedding feast or will you be shut out?

YHWH is in the process of restoring His people and preparing them for the promised great regathering. Just as the Children of Yisrael were separated, protected and delivered from the bondage of Egypt through the Appointed Times in the midst of judgment, the same is about to occur again, only on a global scale.

In fact, this future deliverance will make the past exodus from Egypt pale in comparison.[165] Just as the mixed multitude in Egypt was gathered along with

---
[165] Jeremiah 16:14-15

Yisrael, so will a Covenant people from all the nations be gathered to YHWH. This will occur at the end of the age when the nations are judged as described in the Book of Revelation.

This truth has been obscured and hidden due to religions and denominational factions interpreting the Scriptural texts to suit their own agenda. It is time for those who desire truth to shed the traditions of man that have been heaped upon them and begin to undergo restoration and a return to the ways of YHWH.

This book is an attempt to aid truth seekers in that process. As such, it should not be viewed as an attack on any religion or denomination, but rather a call to restoration for those who are drawn to the voice of the Messiah and recognize that they have inherited lies.

If you are a Christian and are feeling defensive that is only natural. The truths contained in this book may be shocking. In some instances they completely contradict the traditions that are being taught in mainstream Christianity.

It is a humbling experience to realize that you have been deceived to such an extent. It is also a real eye opener to recognize the degree of cunning and stealth exercised by the adversary. The battle for the souls of mankind is raging while most are completely oblivious and deluded to the extent of the deception and the reality of its existence.

As people daily busy themselves with the cares of the world, they are being choked like seeds that have fallen among the thorns.[166] It certainly makes you appreciate the cleverness of the adversary. The same serpent that deceived Adam and Hawah continues to cast his spell on mankind and he wants to destroy you through your religion.

The modern Christian religion clearly lacks the

---

[166] See Matthew 13, Mark 4 and Luke 8

power demonstrated by the early Assembly because they fail to fully understand the Scriptures or the power of Elohim.[167] This is due to the fact that the Christian religion has generally rejected the standard of righteousness set forth in the Torah and has mixed with the pagan traditions of the world.

Christianity teaches that a person who obeys the righteous instructions of the Torah is legalistic. This creates an incredible paradox for Christians because the Torah is considered to be wisdom and understanding for the Covenant people. It is intended for the Bride, to set her apart from the nations and allow her to approach YHWH. It is supposed to be diligently obeyed by those in a Covenant relationship with YHWH.[168]

This has never changed and the Messiah came as a shepherd to gather His flock and restore them to the purity of the Torah through the Renewed Covenant. The early followers of Yahushua were Torah observant Yisraelites. They kept the Commandments of Elohim and they had the testimony of Yahushua. They were able to receive the infilling of the Holy Spirit because they were set apart – qadosh. As a result, they could operate in the power of the Spirit.

This will be the same characteristic of the true servants in the end as they return to the

---

[167] This was the same rendered upon the Pharisees by Yahushua who did not believe in the resurrection. See Matthew 22:29 and Mark 12:24.

[168] "⁵ Surely I have taught you statutes and judgments, just as YHWH my Elohim commanded me, that you should act according to them in the land which you go to possess. ⁶ Therefore be careful to observe them; for this is your wisdom and your understanding in the sight of the peoples who will hear all these statutes, and say, Surely this great nation is a wise and understanding people. ⁷ For what great nation is there that has Elohim so near to it, as YHWH our Elohim is to us, for whatever reason we may call upon Him? ⁸ And what great nation is there that has such statutes and righteous judgments as are in all this Torah which I set before you this day? ⁹ Only take heed to yourself, and diligently keep yourself, lest you forget the things your eyes have seen, and lest they depart from your heart all the days of your life. And teach them to your children and your grandchildren, 10 especially concerning the day you stood before YHWH your Elohim in Horeb, when YHWH said to me, Gather the people to Me, and I will let them hear My words, that they may learn to fear Me all the days they live on the earth, and that they may teach their children." (Deuteronomy 4:5-10)

Commandments. They will also have the right to, once again, partake of the Tree of Life.[169]

This was why the disciples maintained the ritual of "baptism," better known as "immersion."[170] When a person repented, the immersion symbolized a cleansing from sin and a crossing over from death to life – from Babylon to Yisrael.

The point was to get clean by the blood of the Lamb of Elohim and then stop sinning. Entering into the Covenant meant joining the Kingdom of YHWH, and the Torah is the constitution of that Kingdom. The Torah defines sin and reveals the righteous conduct that YHWH expects from us.

As a result, after receiving salvation by grace, we need to follow the Torah and exercise righteous living. The Set Apart Spirit will not dwell in a defiled temple. The early Believers could readily receive the Set Apart Spirit because they understood the need to live righteously.[171]

Remember that the first major outpouring of the Spirit described in the Book of Acts occurred at the Appointed Time known as Shavuot.[172] Those who were in Jerusalem in obedience to the Commandments were in the right place at the right time to receive the message of the Good News in their own language as the Spirit gave

---

[169] Revelation 12:17, 14:12 and 22:14

[170] The immersion process was an integral part of meeting with YHWH at His House. All would immerse, which symbolized a cleansing from sin, before entering into His presence and doing business with Him.

[171] According to the Book of Acts, new converts were given certain preliminary Commandments to obey with the understanding that Moses (the Torah) was read in the Synagogues every Sabbath. (Acts 15:21). In other words, they were given certain immediate instructions to get them cleaned up from the defilements of the pagan lives that they were coming out of. (Acts 15:19-20). They were then expected to attend the Synagogue and learn the Torah each week. They could then continue to apply the righteous commandments to their lives as needed. This advice was deemed good by the elders and the Holy (Set Apart) Spirit. (Acts 15:28).

[172] Christianity calls this Appointed Time "Pentecost," but it is Shavuot in Hebrew – the Feast of Weeks. It is an important time after the grain harvest when the firstfruits are gathered to the House of YHWH. It is a rehearsal intended to prepare those in Covenant with YHWH for the Great Harvest at the end of the age.

utterance.

It is no coincidence that this was the same Appointed Time when YHWH spoke the Commandments before the Set Apart Assembly at Mount Sinai centuries earlier. The relationship between the Torah and the Spirit is inseparable and those who worship YHWH must worship in Spirit and in Truth (Torah).[173]

Many Christians get defensive when presented with this information. It upsets the paradigm that we all inherited, but is also tests the heart. You see nothing in this book is an attack on a person's faith in the Messiah. In fact, this book should build your faith in Messiah by clarifying His role, His purpose and your proper response. It is a challenge to the many traditions that we have learned through religions that deviate from the truth.

After Yisrael left Egypt and eventually crossed the Jordan River under the command of Joshua (Yahushua) they were brought to Shechem. It was there that they renewed the Covenant through Yahushua. This was a pattern that would be repeated by the Messiah. At Shechem they were visibly presented with a choice - obedience and blessing or disobedience and curses. They were told to choose life or death.

Yahushua the Messiah is leading us on that same journey of faith. He tells us to repent, which means to turn back to the Commandments. Christianity claims to follow the Messiah but it rejects His teachings, His Commandments and His Renewed Covenant. As a result, Yahushua does not know Christians who refuse to obey Him - even those who think they know Him and think that they are serving Him.

We will all stand before Yahushua some day and give an account. At that point, there will be no religion,

---

[173] John 4:23. The Torah is specifically defined as truth in Psalm 119:142.

church, tradition or pastor to defend you. If He does not know you then He has already told you your fate. Before that moment of judgment occurs you have an important choice to make – will you follow and obey the Messiah or will you follow the traditions and teachings of a religion that claims to represent Him?

This is indeed the Christian conundrum.

The Walk in the Light Series

Book 1 — Restoration - A discussion of the pagan influences that have mixed with the true faith through the ages, which has resulted in the need for restoration. This book also examines true Scriptural restoration.

Book 2 — Names - Discusses the True Name of the Creator and the Messiah as well as the significance of names in the Scriptures.

Book 3 — The Scriptures - Discusses the ways that the Creator has communicated with Creation. It also examines the origin of the written Scriptures as well as the various types of translation errors in Bibles that have led to false doctrines in some mainline religions.

Book 4 — Covenants - Discusses the progressive covenants between the Creator and His Creation as described in the Scriptures which reveals His plan for mankind.

Book 5 — The Messiah - Discusses the prophetic promises and fulfillments of the Messiah and the True identity of the Redeemer of Yisrael.

Book 6 — The Redeemed - Discusses the relationship between Christianity and Judaism and reveals how the Scriptures identify True Believers. It reveals how the Christian doctrine of Replacement Theology has caused confusion as to how the Creator views the Children of Yisrael.

Book 7 — The Law and Grace - Discusses in depth the false doctrine that Grace has done away with the Law and demonstrates the vital importance of obeying the commandments.

Book 8 — The Sabbath - Discusses the importance of the Seventh Day Sabbath as well as the origins of the

	tradition concerning Sunday worship.
Book 9	Kosher - Discusses the importance of eating food prescribed by the Scriptures as an aspect of righteous living.
Book 10	Appointed Times - Discusses the appointed times established by the Creator, often erroneously considered to be "Jewish" holidays, and critical to the understanding of prophetic fulfillment of the Scriptural promises.
Book 11	Pagan Holidays - Discusses the pagan origins of some popular Christian holidays which have replaced the Appointed Times.
Book 12	The Final Shofar - Examines the ancient history of the earth and prepares the Believer for the deceptions coming in the end of the age. Also discusses the walk required by the Scriptures to be an overcomer and endure to the end.

To order any of the books in the Walk in the Light Series in print or ebook format visit:

www.shemayisrael.net

The Shema
Deuteronomy (Debarim) 6:4-5

Traditional English Translation

Hear, O Israel: The LORD our God, the LORD is one! You shall love the LORD your God with all your heart, with all your soul, and with all your strength.

Corrected English Translation

Hear, O Yisrael: YHWH our Elohim, YHWH is one (unified)!
You shall love YHWH your Elohim with all your heart, with all your soul, and with all your strength.

Modern Hebrew Text

שְׁמַע ישראל יהוה אלהינו יהוה אחד
את יהוה אלהיך בכל- לבבך ובכל- נפשך ובכל- מאדך
ואהבת

Ancient Hebrew Text

⊲ᴀ× ᴈᴨᴈɏ ᴨɏɏᴈᏨ× ᴈᴨᴈɏ Ϛ×ᴖʍɏ ⊙ʍw
ᴀᴖᴖϚ-Ϛɏᴖ ᴀɏᴈϚ× ᴈᴨᴈɏ ×× ×ᴖᴈ×ɏ
ᴀ⊲×ʍ-Ϛɏᴖɏ ᴀwᴖɏ-Ϛɏᴖɏ

Hebrew Text Transliterated

Shema, Yisra'el: YHWH Elohenu, YHWH echad!
V-ahavta et YHWH Elohecha b-chol l'bacha u-b-chol naf'sh'cha u-b-chol m'odecha.

The Shema has traditionally been one of the most important prayers in Judaism and has been declared the first (resheet) of all the Commandments. (Mark 12:29-30).

www.ingramcontent.com/pod-product-compliance
Lightning Source LLC
Chambersburg PA
CBHW070458100426
42743CB00010B/1676